KARMA ROAD

Walking Through Time
with George Eliot

A true story of synchronicity,
parallel lives, & reincarnation

Freda M. Chaney, D.D.

∞

Astley Book Farm
August 2014
see p 346)

Book cover design by Freda M. Chaney

Front cover photo of Astley Church gate by Norman Chaney

Book interior design by Freda M. Chaney

ISBN-13: 978-1508635826

ISBN-10: 150863582x

For my family with love and deep gratitude.

∞

Contents

Part 3   Unleashing the Lunacy

Appendix

Foreword

Y ou are in for a treat! This book you are holding is inspiring, uplifting, and thought provoking! Within the first few pages you are given a key to unlock the compelling record of the author's encounter with herself in a previous life. Keep your key handy, there are several doors to pass through in this amazing account right up to the last page! If you deny reincarnation is real, keep reading and your doubts will likely be dispelled.

My connection with this author began in 2009. During a visit at the hometown of the famed Brazilian healer known as "John of God," I received an email through my website contact form from a person by the name of Freda Chaney. She introduced herself as a Doctor of Divinity graduate from the American Institute of Holistic Theology. She had viewed *Orbs: The Veil is Lifting* DVD, and had read *The Orb Project*. She said she had a collection of orb and other anomaly photos, and offered to share her photos if it would help advance my efforts in orb study.

In my response to Freda, I asked that she email one photo to me—the most pertinent one "where you strongly feel that the orb in the picture is telling a message." I asked that she accompany it with a narrative that would elaborate on the circumstances under which the photo was taken. I also suggested a description of what her mind was focusing on when she took the photo, and how she would interpret the situation.

What she decided to send me was so remarkable that it changed her life in a profound way. As well, it changed my own views about reincarnation! It was a photo showing an orb perched atop a book on a shelf in her private library. Freda noted that it contained the faces of two female persons. I was able to substantiate this for myself after image processing, including strong magnification. Freda described that, following her husband's advice, she picked up the book on which the orb had appeared. It was a book she had never read by an author who wasn't among her favorites.

Leafing through the book, Freda found several parallels between the protagonist and her own life. This, of course, spurred her curiosity, and she read the book from cover to cover, finding numerous additional parallels. She would communicate her findings to me, and I would make remarks or pose follow-up questions. An intense email exchange regarding what came to be known as *The Mill on the Floss* Project, ensued over a period of several months. Following the publication of *The Orb Project*, which I co-authored with Dr. Miceal Ledwith, I had been working jointly with my wife, Gundi Heinemann, on a sequel book, focusing on the potential meaning behind the orb phenomenon, and investigating if there are messages the orbs want to tell us, and how they would go about doing this. Freda's orb story became an intriguing piece of that puzzle, in particular her indisputable identification of the two faces in the orbs' interiority.

She was able to send me another photo taken of the same scene just moments prior to the one that showed the orb on *The Mill on the Floss* book. My evaluation yielded startling conclusions about the intelligence underlying the appearance of orbs on photos. In our book published by Hay House, *Orbs: Their Mission and Messages of Hope*, Freda's initial story and our shared findings are discussed in detail.

Freda's primary interest was based on the increasingly intriguing parallels she had discovered between George Eliot and herself. She studied every book by the author she could find, and reviewed AIHT textbooks about reincarnation which she had read as a student. Was Freda a reincarnation of George Eliot?

This question precipitated the search that would evolve from being an object of academic interest for Freda, to her own personal involvement through the entanglement of George Eliot's life with her own. The question advanced from the status of an object of interest to the subject of a quest. She uncovered serious health-related parallels between George Eliot and herself. The answers could be an issue of survival. She just had to find out what all this meant for her life.

In this book, *Karma Road*, Freda describes how she discovered that she had been reliving the life of the Victorian period author. What had started with one simple orb photo, evolved into the realization of a lifetime. In the ultimate analysis, the orb that appeared on *The Mill on the Floss* book may have prolonged Freda's health and wellbeing, and perhaps saved her life.

Freda Chaney is an intelligent, talented writer with the wonderful gift of being able to share what she has discovered in a fascinating and elementary way. The reader will be reluctant to put her book down from the first chapter to the last. Why? Because the subject is a deep, timeless mystery about each of us. Have we lived before? And if so, who have we been? These questions are left to you at book's end. Only you can answer them for yourself, but thankfully, you have been given a key.

Freda's story brought to the surface a question for my own life. Is it time to inquire more thoroughly into the significance of a possible past life of my own? Had I been a certain 17th century Italian composer and organist as I'd been told years ago? And if so, what relevance might it hold for me in my current life?

~ Klaus Heinemann, Ph.D.

The Orb Project, Beyond Words/Atria Books, 2007; *Orbs: Their Mission and Messages of Hope*, Hay House, 2010; *Expanding Perception: Rediscovering the Grand Original Design*, ISBN 10: 1492910805; ISBN 13: 978-1492910800 by Klaus Heinemann with Gundi Heinemann, CreateSpace-Amazon, 2013.

∞

Introduction

We are divine beings walking through time on a karmic road. We have the power as individuals to evolve—to recreate our lives regardless of current or past life karma. This is the reason for, and the hope of, the reincarnated soul. We are all in this karmic soup together. If we are human, we have karma.

This shocking, true story is an in-depth study of the parallels between my life and the life of the famous nineteenth century novelist, George Eliot. I invite you to set aside any closed notions you may have about reincarnation, karma, even religion in general. Please keep an open mind until you have read the entire book. The world in which we live is not just what we can see. It is what we *can't* see that will open our eyes!

I am not an Eliot scholar or critic. I seek only to tell my story about the many parallels between us, what I learned about myself while researching Eliot's life, and how I overcame karma that was threatening my wellbeing as it had threatened hers.

What does this book have to do with you? Everything! Ask yourself these questions. Who are you? What are you doing with your life—your time? When will you take action to release the karma that keeps recycling experiences through the law of cause and effect? Why are you here? The answer to the final question is that you are on a journey to the self. You are a soul pioneer.

Karma Road will help you live deliberately. Stories help us live meaningful lives. We read them in ancient Scriptures, plays, poetry, novels, motivational books, blogs, magazines, newspapers, and on social sites. Our stories weave past, present, and future. They help us learn to honor the eternal soul, and begin to evolve into patterns of wellbeing. We aren't stuck unless we choose to be. How divine!

The "Quick Parallels List" appears in Appendix A at the back of this book. My list began in 2009, and has multiplied to nearly one hundred parallels. I have recorded seventy of them in this book list.

Karma Road is divided into three sections. Part I introduces and explores the possibilities of a parallel life or reincarnation. Part II contains commentary on three of George Eliot's books, one novella, and an essay about the "common" in art and poetry, juxtaposing them with my own life and work. Part III concludes my story, healing the past, present, and future.

George Eliot used several names during her lifetime.* They are listed below as an aid to the reader. When I refer to George Eliot, generally it encompasses all of these names as the adult person, and other times it specifically refers to the author after she started using her pen name. I suggest the reader refer to this guide as needed for clarification.

1 Mary Anne Evans from 1819 as recorded in her father's journal at her baptism.

2 Mary Ann Evans during her childhood, young adult years at boarding school, and early adult life.

3 Marian Evans from 1851, her chosen professional name.

4 Marian Evans-Lewes from 1854, her chosen name while living with Lewes.

5 George Eliot from 1859, her pseudonym for writing.

6 Mary Ann Cross from 1880, upon marrying John Walter Cross.

* The Information above includes names and dates as they are published in Rosemary Ashton's *George Eliot* by Oxford University Press *Very Interesting People* series, 2007.

Part 1

∞ Parallels through Time ∞

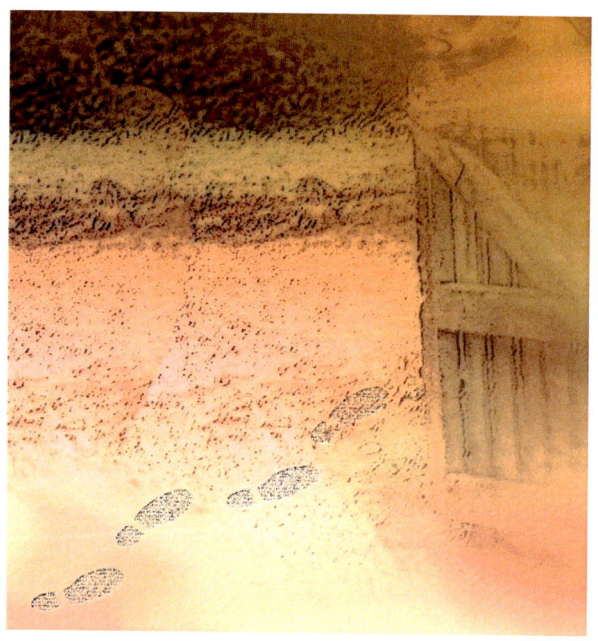

-1-

The Spirit of a House

When I was six, I was old enough to realize my childhood was probably over! My mother, who would have molded me into a lovely representation of herself, was dead. She was replaced by a church-going mother of one would-be sister for me. There was a quick annulment. Then came a sixteen-year-old Elizabeth Taylor look-alike with a baby of her own. She moved in as a fulltime sitter, and married my father in 1960. She talked about her terrible childhood, curses, and how I might die because the bird hit the window in the room where I slept. There was a deep mystery surrounding her, and strange things began to happen. She said she saw my mother's ghost and that we'd have to move. We moved twice in two years. Maybe Mom was following us! My mother's family was banished from our midst. But for a rare visit from a brave soul who felt led to speak on my mother's behalf, I would not see my maternal relatives again until I was fourteen years old.

I was always the first to admit my family was different. It was common for my dad to purposely scare me. He would drag his leg like a zombie, squint up one eye, drop his false teeth, and chase me around the house. He repeatedly reminded me that he would haunt me when he died. My stepmother claimed to "know" things, and there were always horror movies playing on the TV. My brothers and I watched Chiller Theater every weekend. Every Saturday night was like Halloween at our house. Sugary treats were brought into the living room, and we ate ourselves comatose as the *Night of the Living Dead* movie piped over the Pittsburgh channel. I often had nightmares. I didn't blame my parents. They did the best they could with what they had. They had no clue things might have been better.

In primary schools of the 1960s, students were given a Gideon's Bible, and there in our little Midwest town, I got mine. Tucking it securely under the covers of my bed during the day, and holding it in my hungry hands at night, that little red New Testament took me through most of my young adult years as the house collected horror shows, whining country music, and a line-up of mysteries and drama from the lifestyle we led. I couldn't wait to leave. I stayed prayed up, hoping the ghosts wouldn't follow me when I left. At eighteen, I was married and living in my own home. At nineteen I delivered my beautiful gray-eyed daughter. When she smiled, I saw my mother's eyes—the ones that looked all glassy like pretty marbles that defy dust. The ghost had not followed, but the family traits had.

Joining my husband's church, I learned that I had to give up Christmas—the only redemption the year offered when I was young. During my childhood, there was magic for a month. The soap camels trekked across white cotton hillocks, the chipped Wise Men stared at the stars in hopes of being made whole, the silver tinsel that seemed kitsch any other time of year was glorious then. Being robbed of it ripped me! Religion was not my thing—not a real way of life. Having a bunch of "oughts" to keep in life seemed silly somehow. It would not save the starving children in China!

I wanted to know what love was, and I hurt myself and many others who entered my path in the process of learning. I was looking for love and security. Everyone was looking for love, but sometimes people look for security and mistake it for love. At least I was not guilty of the latter. I loved the men I married. I simply could not cope. The very thing I desired became my master time and again. I needed control of my life, but married controllers. I was a motherless daughter— vulnerable. My mother was lost to me, but it was no excuse not to find myself. It was a long struggle through time, relationships, and circumstances.

Several decades later, I was settled and satisfied with my life. I'd made it through several careers of my choice, my daughter was grown and happily married, and I could still count the number of my failed serious relationships with men on one hand. I'd saved the best for last. My marriage to Norm worked because we pulled in tandem. We both had Scottish roots and had grown up in farming country. We loved books and educated ourselves about life beyond our common gates. Norm guided, but had no need to control me. He had control of himself and knew the direction of his own life. I admired how he was perfectly satisfied with who he was as a person. Ours was an abiding love in which we both understood what we had to give to the relationship to make it special. We had fun—great fun! We made mistakes and forgave one another. We were best friends.

Life was more than I had hoped for in the sleepy little town where my husband and I operated our historical bed and breakfast. I blessed the house the day we first arrived. Out came the oil and the holy water. I walked from room to room and repeated Bible scriptures as I tossed droplets. This was going to be the perfect haven for guests to come, to read in the large west library, to hear the angel stories that I had experienced and shared through *Angels on Earth* magazine and *Guideposts for Kids*. Living the blessings and blessing the living daily was not religion. It was more like *Little House on the Prairie*. I could do that!

But soon, my life would change forever. My house offered-up something that jolted memories from many years before.

"I think we have spirits!"

"What are you saying, dear? Of course we have spirits! Calm down, and start from the beginning." I was shivering from top to bottom, but somehow I managed to gather myself together so that I could tell Norm the whole story—what I could understand of it anyway.

"I mean disembodied spirits! You see, I was back in the library taking photographs of the book case. I uploaded the photos, and in one I saw a glowing ball of light situated on top of a book. It has faces in it!"

"Have you been drinking? Getting sufficient sleep?"

"No and yes! The photo tells the story! Look!"

"That is interesting," Norm said calmly. "Which book is that glowing ball resting upon?" He was like a stone, not changing his position in his favorite brown tweed chair.

"Seriously, Norm! What does the book have to do with it?"

"Precisely!" Norm could be infuriatingly calm, to the point, and sharp as Occam's razor at cutting away the unnecessary. "Go get it. Have a look. See what it is trying to tell you."

"OK, I will!" Sheepishly, I walked back to the library, turning on all of the lights as I went through the music room. It's dark and brooding silence only came to life when we lit the chandelier and sat at the mahogany baby grand piano, or entertained guests at the Queen Anne style dining table. I lingered momentarily in the luxury of the deep rose carpet held to the original chestnut flooring by dark antique and reproduction furniture. It was not my favorite room, but it had its purpose for entertainment. I much preferred bright rooms with windows that offered up a sense of serenity like a Vermeer painting. I surrounded the music room with angel statues to offer a feeling of redemption. The marble bar invited me for a glass of brandy. I could use one after the twilight feeling the photo had just revealed to me!

No, I needed my senses about me, so I moved on through the hallway where the spiral cherry staircase was like a lift to heaven. Nothing was lovelier in our home. Original to the 1823 manor house, its graceful curve of seventeen stairs led up to the master rooms joined by a wide hall. A wallpaper border wound like a ribbon around the impressive spindled staircase. Its Pug dog motif lent Victorian charm to the counter balanced colors of deep scarlet and hunter green that dominated the hall and staircase. Generous six-over-six pane windows created patterns of light at sunset, casting sacred shadows onto the wall winding like a castle turret to the first floor.

The ground floor would have offered a parlor to be sure. Entering through the massive front door, one would first see the winding staircase as in the Andrew Jackson Hermitage House and other houses of the period. There was an overwhelming urge to walk to the right into the parlor, or as we knew it today, the library. My mind began to wander, and I could almost sense the way the room might have looked in the 1800s. I had to ratchet-down my creative urges and get on with the task at hand.

I moved through the hallway and into the dark library. The blues and greens of the room, coupled with the dark furniture, offered a sense of male mastery and increased my feelings of intrigue about the room. Had this been the room where the original master of the house sat and read books just as we were doing now?

I held the strange photograph in front of me and tracked the book's location on the shelf. It was George Eliot's novel, *The Mill on the Floss* in the exact position on the shelf where the glowing ball had been. I pulled the book down from the shelf. My hands were shaking as though this very moment had the potential to change my entire life! Was Eliot trying to tell me something? Oh, I didn't really believe in ghosts, but I did believe the spirit survives the death of the body. I studied reincarnation and karma for my divinity degree, but the jury was still out for me. And if I even hinted that I was looking into other truths not mentioned in the Holy Bible, my family, my Midwest neighbors, my lifelong friends would think me a heretic. It would not be the first time. But this Eliot lady, this nineteenth century novelist, had my head spinning and not for a Catholic exorcism!

Uncasing the heavy volume, I found a maroon cloth bound cover embossed with a beautiful gold leaf cottage flanked by a mill wheel spilling water. Somehow this image was familiar to me. I turned the pages slowly and was delighted to find numerous paintings by Wray Manning throughout the book. Leafing through, I felt somehow haunted by the images, as though I already knew the story before reading it! Slowly I began to introduce myself to the history of Mary Ann (George Eliot before she took her pen name) and her family by reading the enclosed monthly newsletter, *The Heritage Club Sandglass,* and the Introduction to the Heritage Edition of *The Mill on the Floss* by David Daiches.

Mary Ann's father, Robert Evans, was the manager for the Newdigate family who owned the estate on which Griff House stood. Mary Ann would sometimes ride with him to the Newdigates' gothic style Arbury Hall nearby and enjoy the thousands of books in the extravagantly decorated library. Mary Ann borrowed as many books as she could carry in her arms back home to Griff. Many of those books found their way to the sitting room where the family gathered in front of the fireplace to read and share news of the day, and in Mary Ann's own room on a bed stand where she read well into the night.

Surely books were savored in the attic near her favorite window. I can just see the gray-eyed Mary Ann leaning through the attic window summoning the sun for a beautiful day of fishing with her brother, Isaac. And if, by chance, the sun did not penetrate the stubborn Midlands cloud layer allowing for a play day with her brother, Mary Ann would turn to her imagination and dream of Sir Walter Scott adventures, acting them out in the dusty rafters of the Griff House attic. She possessed a creative imagination that would not quit. I could identify with that.

My mind was reeling. What could I possibly have in common with this writer? Writing? Creativity? Curiosity? Or something deeper, like karma? I read somewhere that karma can be housed, that souls can carry energy imprints into several succeeding lifetimes, and that they tend to return to places where they have lived in order to work out unfinished business. Thankfully, our house had positive karmic vibes. The moment I first saw our manor house I had the sense that it was more than just mortar and bricks. It had a heart. I pictured planting an herb garden, creating a perfect space for meditation, and adding statuary that would take on a life of its own after a few years of watching over hallowed ground. Our home was built in 1823, an imposing red brick house that is much like the manor style farmhouses of nineteenth century England.

Young Mary Ann lived in such a house where her family moved shortly following her birth in 1819. The Griff House was a red brick stronghold for family dreams. Mary Ann Evans lived out her childhood and early adulthood creating, unknowingly, books in her imagination. The most important work to come from her Griff House memories was *The Mill on the Floss*, the very book on which I'd found the glowing ball of light! Mary Ann loved Griff house, and that love left an indelible mark on her soul. I searched the Internet for pictures of the Griff House. What was not to love? A winding drive led to the front door of the sprawling brick house. The front wasn't particularly fancy, but very strong like a reliable man. It had a thick, simple front door with a mail slot of brass. Generous windows with high arches softened her face during harsh Warwickshire winters and peeked out through the ivy that clung to her frames during the mild Midlands summers.

I knew that the possessions inside a home create an even stronger energy impression. I studied for years to learn what creates mood and comfort in living spaces. I applied that knowledge to my home. Most rooms in our manor house have several chairs for reading, and books are ever-present enticing readers to dig in and create magic for their own lives. Young Mary Ann Evans loved books in a way most people cannot begin to imagine. They were her life! And now they are mine. It was clear to me that Mary Ann had many opportunities to enjoy riches beyond her own family's home by roaming Arbury Hall, but she adored living at the Griff House. I believe part of her heart remained after she moved to Foleshill, Coventry when her brother, Isaac, married and took over the Griff House and farm. Loving my country home as I do, I could imagine her feelings of homesickness.

Our manor house was a bed and breakfast in the front and private living quarters in the back. Many a day had been spent in the front of the house having tea in delicate Haviland China cups, while reading the poetry of the great Romantics: Keats, Byron, Shelly. Norm was particularly fond of Shakespeare's verse, so from time to time we would read some of his sonnets. It was there in the front of the house—in the west library—where the ball of light chose Eliot's book! Christmas had come and gone. Guests had arrived, admired the surroundings, and reluctantly departed. My camera in hand, I had made my way through the house to take photos of the Christmas decorations before I packed them away. In the dark, womb-like library, my eyes had been drawn to the book shelves. "Someday I will read all of these books," I promised myself.

"Is everything ok?" Norm said leaning around the corner of the door to peer into the library.

"You scared me nearly to death!" I screeched.

"Did you think I was the ghost of the library?"

"Funny!" I held up the book, and Norm walked closer to have a look.

"Ah yes, George Eliot! I know her novel, *Middlemarch*, but I am unfamiliar with this one. He thumbed through and stopped momentarily to look at the paintings. Looks interesting. Will you read it?"

"I should. I mean it doesn't look like an uncommonly exciting book, and yet, it does seem to draw me in. I love the cover and colorful interior paintings."

"You should have a go at it. Find out what the experience is trying to tell you," Norm said. He patted me on the shoulder and turned to leave the room.

"Yes, professor!" I said jokingly, remembering a time and place where Norm did not know me from the next student, a time when I was just another name on his grade book, a shy flower that would hardly speak in class. He put red marks across my papers and left notes in the margins suggesting how I might improve my writing. I fretted over the assignments more than most. At that time, poetry was my life. Each word was significant—each metaphor was mindful. I often pictured Norm in my mind with his red pen sweeping the page like Zorro with his whip. Suddenly, I felt vulnerable. I felt like running away and not reading the book, but something told me I was unable to turn back now. I *had* to read it! After all, my husband, the professor, thought I should.

I had never cared for Eliot's writings. Even with her book sitting on a prominent library shelf overlooking a burgundy hardbound collection of Charles Dickens (with whom Eliot and her soulmate had shared conversation), Eliot had not caught my attention. Until now! So no one is more surprised than I to be summoned by this leftover energy named George Eliot! There is a quote attributed to her, "It is never too late to be what you might have been." I can apply that quote directly to myself! It was never too late to read George Eliot novels, and to learn from her the ropes of tangled relationships and how to untangle them through writing! I'd been writing for over forty years, and my writing had won awards, but I hadn't dug the well deeply enough. Perhaps now was the time to do so—now that the glowing anomaly had made a special effort to point out Eliot's book.

Some call these round lights "orbs." I'd seen them before in my digital photographs, but never one that had two faces in it! Some thought orbs to be nothing more than dust particles. Others conjectured that they were moisture. And there were those who feared they were ghosts! But a handful of experts believed them to be "messengers" who were around to assist us! In my case it would seem the latter, since the light had targeted one book, *The Mill on the Floss.* So began my literary journey from my library in the rolling rural heartland of the Midwest U.S. to the hauntingly beautiful

Warwickshire countryside in the Midlands of England through the writings of Eliot. As I read, I recorded each parallel between Eliot and me. I wondered if I was doing this for myself and Norm, or for someone out there who needed to hear the mysterious story that was unfolding in front of me. Perhaps both. At that moment as I stood in the library feeling sorry for myself, I felt that most people couldn't give a fig about such bizarre information. I needed some friends and mentors to guide me in this mission to solve the mystery.

Suddenly, it occurred to me that I needed to make contact with someone who studied orbs. I looked for books on Amazon, and I quickly discovered one from Atria Books titled *The Orb Project*. I ordered it and a DVD that was listed as well titled, *ORBS: The Veil is Lifting*. The co-authors of the book were serious about their findings. But my friends and family would think I'd lost my mind if I spoke of seeing orbs in my photographs! I read the book and watched the DVD. I was convinced I needed to introduce my story to one person in particular, Klaus Heinemann, Ph.D. He was a physicist who had sixty peer reviewed papers to his credit. He had done research at NASA, and was a research professor at Stanford University. He had written his own books about consciousness and perception. It was a big leap from Dr. Heinemann's professional background to co-authoring a book about orbs, and that intrigued me. It would have intrigued Eliot too.

I wrote to Dr. Heinemann telling him about the orb on *The Mill on the Floss* book and offered the photo for his research. He immediately wrote back requesting the photo with the orb perched atop the book, and in addition, the photo before and/or after that particular photo. I sent the photos to him, beginning what we came to refer to as "*The Mill on the Floss* Project," which lasted for several months.

The results of the research were to be published as an introduction to my story in Klaus and Gundi Heinemann's book, *ORBS: Their Mission and Messages of Hope*. My search did not end there. I continued to find dozens of parallels between Eliot and me. I knew that she had something for me to tell—to publish for modern readers. So I took copious notes, and joined the George Eliot Fellowship in England to do some research on this mysterious author who used a man's name and rejected organized religion. I knew in my heart that I would someday visit the Griff House where she grew up. It was just a matter of when.

During my long hours of reading, I learned the ultimate pain of George Eliot's lifetime from one paragraph in Book 1 of *The Mill on the Floss*:

We learn to restrain ourselves as we grow older. We keep apart when we have quarreled, express ourselves in well-bred phrases, and in this way preserve a dignified alienation, showing much firmness on one side, and swallowing much grief on the other.

Mary Ann Evans was to stay briefly at the Griff House one last time in 1850 following her father's death, but family disagreements would prevent her from returning with any sense of appreciation. She moved on, staying with good friends at their Rosehill estate on the outskirts of Coventry. These friends left a deep imprint on Mary Ann's future. She later moved to London where the busy work of editing helped her cope with the beehive of bad memories that stung her soul-deep. Still, the negativity surrounding the disintegration of her relationship with her family would forever remain upon her heart to become karma spilling into future—perhaps my future!

I may be possessed, but not with a wayward spirit! I am driven by this mysterious person who is perhaps me in another time and place! George Eliot, the Victorian female novelist, who wrote under a male pseudonym, has piqued my interest to say the least. I will hunt her down, cry over her father's crypt, argue with her brother, visit her childhood home, gaze at her photos, and make magnanimous efforts to feel what she felt. She might even enjoy the crazy things I do like flying in a bi-wing plane while wearing an Amelia Earhart jacket and leather aviator hat. But I am also a bookworm, so we can share books. After all, Eliot already knew her way around my library.

–2–

Familiar Fathers

If there is such a thing as karmic overload, there must be a modern solution—a karmic detox to expunge the negative soul imprint of this literary maven. When my Eliot drama began in 2009, days would pass unnoticed as I immersed myself in *The Mill on the Floss*. I had always loved Jane Austen's work, so at first I had to force myself to read George Eliot. I was soon to learn that I felt right at home with her books. I was hoping something I learned through reading her work could unlock the mysterious link between the Victorian novelist and me. While I still clung like an heir to Austen, I felt that somehow Eliot held the key to my life.

The parallels between George Eliot and me are many, and granted, *The Mill on the Floss* was no thrilling piece of literary work, but it held me like a steel trap because it was telling a literary version of my own life story. I studied a picture of a Wray Manning painting in the Heritage Edition of *The Mill on the Floss* featuring two females seated together. The one on the left had a light complexion and was wearing a light dress. The one on the right had a dark complexion and was wearing a dark dress with a white collar. Comparing this picture to the orb photo, I found that the two were, indeed, similar. *The Mill on the Floss* was an autobiographical account of Mary Ann Evan's life with her family. The two females in the picture had to be Maggie and Lucy. Mary Ann was represented by the character, Maggie. The character Lucy, Maggie's cousin in the book, was based on Mary Ann's older sister, Chrissy. So, not only could the orb "ladies" represent the characters of Maggie and Lucy, but also Mary Ann and her older sister, Chrissy. Plausible.

It was unsettling, dredging up the similarities between the arrogant character, Tom, in the novel and Eliot's real life older brother, Isaac, who was rigid in his ways, but close to Mary Ann during their childhood. I was also very close to my younger brother as a child, and had been separated from him because of misunderstandings. He and I were closer in birth order, so we were like twins exploring the woods on our farm, discovering caves and waterfalls together, walking on our bare feet to an old fashioned grocery store over a mile away. Years and tears separated my brother and me as they had Maggie and Tom in *The Mill on the Floss*. I, like George Eliot and her autobiographical character Maggie, had felt the sting of rejection from family members. Everyone experiences rejection in life. It is part of the human experience. How we handle the rejection is paramount to our success. If we forgive and move on, we grow. If we hold grudges and become negative, we stagnate. Karma, the law of cause and effect, is the vehicle moving the unresolved issues forward, perhaps into the next lifetime. This is one of my life lessons passed down from George Eliot as an energy imprint—the emotional turmoil that had been unresolved for years needed resolution. I was determined to overcome!

I learned that George Eliot chose to represent her father in the novel, *The Mill on the Floss*, as Mr. Tulliver. He was doting and permissive. Maggie could do no wrong, and it was to her father she would run when her brother Tom broke her heart, or when her mother and aunts scolded her. I wish there had been someone for me to run to as a child. Perhaps it was too painful for George Eliot to portray herself in the book as anything but Daddy's perfect little girl. In fact, Mary Ann and her father would have serious disagreements as she entered adulthood. There was a near separation of households when they lived in Foleshill, Coventry. Mary Ann refused to go to church because her views had changed from her earlier habits of being zealous in her Christian walk. They say there is nothing worse than an "ex" anything, and Mary Ann was no exception. She would come to refer to this standoff with her father as the "holy war."

I understood this relationship between Mary Ann and her father perfectly. Her father seemed a mountain of strength; there was nothing he could not do. The same held true for my own father, or so I thought as a child. Like Eliot's father, mine was wise about the ways of the land. He was mostly self-employed, a timber man who cleared the land and sent the timber to sawmills in Eastern Ohio. Eventually, my father started his own sawmill. The only thing that outdid the sharp caw of the crow on a clear morning was the high-pitched whirring of the giant saw blade that was at the center of Dad's operation. One by one the stately trees that had defined our property lay in a heap waiting for the ragged ride on the conveyor belt and the stinging saw blade of the mill. When he learned of coal in the area, Dad taught himself to strip mine. The neighbors winced when heavy equipment came through and moved across the green hills gouging the otherwise serene face of our sixty acre farm. He began to purchase land adjoining our property, and soon he was ripping through the woods, the caves, the streams of my childhood, and taking my heart with it. But Dad was a businessman first, and a bleeding heart second. I had to accept that.

He was a versatile mechanic who could fix anything that had a motor. Our back field was littered with cars he hoped one day to restore. On summer evenings I would stand at the fence line and watch the sun transform the horizon to a deep salmon color, and as if by magic the junk cars disappeared into the passion-pink light. Dad learned carpentry from watching others build. He built his first home and assisted others in building theirs. But most of all, my father enjoyed farming. He worked the land and raised farm animals that became our friends only to be served up on our plates at supper time. Dad knew all about raising and butchering livestock. He would sit for hours and apply ingredients to cure hams that fed us through the long Midwest winters. We sold our eggs and made our own butter as Mary Ann's family had done. When neighbors needed advice, they would come to my father because he knew the old ways of farming that everyone admired. Dad was also successful as a manager in his later years when he was employed by others. Everyone knew, though, not to make my father angry! That was his karma.

The template of my father's life was strikingly similar to Robert Evan's life. Mary Ann's father was a man of much "life knowledge." He knew about timber, and architecture, he knew how to farm the land and raise animals, and he knew the ways of mining that existed around Warwickshire. Mr. Evans would sit in a special place to do his business work. His office area had windows facing the large brick barn near the entrance drive to the Griff property. My father had his own desk near a window that faced the barn at the end of our driveway. They were businessmen, both made of rugged stock, working the land, and sharpening their resolve to always do their best.

Searching online, I found an account in John Cross' *Life and Letters of George Eliot* that tells of a time when Robert Evans was riding on a coach and overheard a woman complain that a "hulking sailor" next to her was being rude. Mr. Evans asked the woman to trade him seats, at which time he grabbed the rascal in question by the collar, threw him under the seat, and held him there until the coach had reached its destination. That was my father too: always coming to the aid of those who were less able to defend themselves, especially women. Mr. Evans was strong, and everyone marveled at how he could lift objects that his farmhands could not. My father was likely smaller than Mr. Evans, but he was mighty!

I was hungry for George Eliot—emotionally and intellectually. She was speaking my life in the words of her novel. I leaned back on my hand-carved Victorian headboard, and closed my eyes to visualize the character, Maggie. *The Mill on the Floss* described her as having dark hair, dark unusual eyes, and dark skin. That description fit my own. The character Maggie was a precocious child born into a family that did not support "high-thinking" in women. I shared that likeness with the character, Maggie. I was a precocious child born into a Midwestern farm family that did not believe in "high-thinking" at all. My father believed a woman's place was, for the most part, keeping house and having babies. As a child, I suspicioned that I had been adopted. I was so different from everyone else in my family that it was sometimes painful to endure.

My father lectured me about being the perfect stay-at-home wife and mother, but if in the event that my husband needed monetary help, I would need to work, with Dad's blessing, outside the home. He was one of twelve children birthed by a woman who worked the fields, baked the best pies in the state, grew vegetables, dressed meats for the local market, and somehow handled her grumpier-than-most husband. Dad told a tale about my grandmother that really had us all wondering. She was said to have birthed a baby in the pea patch, then miraculously stood up and continued picking peas. Though we all have our doubts about the truth of this story, tall tales were a welcome part of our childhood.

Dad was not keen on higher education. He quit school before graduation, so he had no appreciation of the value of a degree. He thought a woman's head should be watching a pot of stew, not reading a book. But it was hopeless—I lived for books and writing. I spoke up more than once about how my life would be different from the proposals he and my stepmother lined up for me. It was a rare event when I did talk back because I knew I would take some knocks for my disrespectful behavior. I had a voice, but it was weak. I had courage, but it was, of necessity, hidden. I had a strong will, and that's what carried me by default most of my life.

Mary Ann's father encouraged her education, feeling she would not receive offers of marriage because of her lack of beauty. He paid private tutors to teach his daughter at home after her mother died. She was a teenager under his thumb, though theirs was a mutual dependence. But eventually, Mary Ann challenged her father to gain some semblance of freedom from his overseeing eye. It would have been unusual in her time for a female to confront the master of the household. Young Mary Ann loved pleasing her father and doted on him, but in desperate times, she found her voice when he became too controlling. They both had to learn the art of compromise.

Later, Mary Ann, at thirty four years old and using the more sophisticated pseudonym of Marian, would transfer her affectionate attention to a soulmate. Between them would be an understanding that they were equals. As a result, her voice, through novels, told the world that men and women ought, for the sake of human decency, to be equals.

Another Victorian writer with a male pseudonym, George Sand, put herself into the thick of things, pants and all— fussy dresses be damned! She, like George Eliot, had a "man's intellect," as Eliot was fond of calling it. Sand could not abide being condescended to by men, in which case Chopin must have been the perfect mate for her. Like many modern women, I have a feminine side that desires to please my mate and keep things on an even keel at home, as well as a side that enjoys a great pair of slacks, a short snifter of brandy, and room to be myself—free of male domination.

–3–

The Calling

All grown-ups warn children of the bad things that can happen to them. Kids learn to keep things to themselves so they can savor the prospect of joy for a time. As an adult, I still had that child within warning me to hold my tongue and savor the Eliot experience. My critics would have to wait for their chance to devour me like overbearing parents with wagging fingers and fierce eyes. With this new calling to discover what Eliot had to say to me, I awoke each day with the anticipation of a Dung Beetle rolling her way through the barnyard of life, ignoring the obvious possibilities of danger from the herd.

I scanned every shelf in our library looking for books written by George Eliot. Norm had several paperbacks in his collection, and of course I treasured the hardbound Heritage Edition of *The Mill on the Floss*. I needed a good biography with pictures. While sorting through our books, I could imagine how young Mary Ann felt searching the shelves of the Arbury Hall library, her eyes diverting now and then to the filigreed ceiling that was glorious enough to stir any young girl's imagination. There would be an oversized World Atlas on a low table near the sofa and chairs. Perhaps she'd thumb through it dreaming of places she'd visit as an adult. Maybe she'd touch the spines of the Shakespeare collection. Her love for books was certainly fostered by many persons, especially her boarding school teachers and private tutors. Her father's role in providing her with opportunities of enrichment is not to be overlooked. It was because Robert Evans was an estate manager for the Newdigate family that Mary Ann was well educated and culturally aware. Had Mary Ann been blessed with a beautiful countenance, her father may have arranged an advantageous marriage instead of a higher education. But alas, his youngest daughter was to make her mind and spirit beautiful with books instead.

We, too, had books in our childhood home: a set of *Encyclopedia Britannica*, books on United States presidents, gardening, livestock care, cookbooks, and a few other common books that could be found in the average Midwest home. The elementary schools I attended had bookmobiles that brought books to students once a month. Anticipating the arrival of the Pepto pink bus had the same effect on me as waiting in line for the red and white ice cream wagon. Ding, ding, ding! I remember checking out the book, *Paddy the Beaver* by Thornton Burgess more than once. I adored nature stories. It was not just the story about woodland animals, but the feel of the book in my hands. It was hardbound and smaller than most books. It felt right perched between my small hands. Standing in front of my bedroom vanity mirror, I'd hold the book just so, propping the pages with my thumb and index finger, pretending to read to my imaginary classroom. The stories were filled with fantasy, and I lived inside of them to overcome the boredom in my secluded world at home. Mary Ann and I were both late readers, but when we caught up, we loved books as most children love dolls and board games. We became the characters we read about. We changed our worlds.

Mary Ann was given to such fantasy when tucked away in the attic of the Griff House. She preferred her privacy. It freed her to create. Perhaps that is how *The Mill on the Floss* began—as playful thoughts under the cobwebbed attic rafters. I was alone much in my childhood as well, being the only daughter in our family, and the odd one who loved books and wrote horrid stories. Fourth grade moved us into chapter books with Ms. Neal. *The Diary of Anne Frank* was one of the books we read that year. To this day, I am mortified about the senseless slaughter of the Jews during World War II. The holocaust *was* real, and it extended around the world to pierce our hearts in that fourth grade classroom. When I moved on to high school, there was a well-stocked library which more than made up for any lack of books at home. It is fascinating to realize how the books I've read have shaped my life. George Eliot was now my teacher, counselor, and sister I never had in this life—the sage that would help guide me with her wisdom and wit through my own life experiences.

Young Mary Ann devoured the Bible, Sir Walter Scott novels, *Aesop's Fables* and other common books of the time. Church was obviously a large part of her education and her early call to duty within the community. My childhood church history consisted of a few visits to a local Methodist church until my father declared it was too much like a funeral. I visited a friendly neighbor to have Bible study with Jehovah's Witnesses who came by regularly. Our own family owned a Bible of course, but it was dustier than most books in the house.

When the Gideons handed out the New Testament in our sixth grade classroom, I read the Psalms and fell in love. Every night I would read in the dim hallway light that shone into my bedroom until my stepmother caught me reading beyond my bedtime! Those Psalms saved me from nightmares, but not from scoldings. Mary Ann's mother fretted over her daughter's "after hours" reading as well. Mrs. Evans worried about Mary Ann's eyesight and her heavy use of candles late at night. Perhaps Mary Ann read to avoid her "night terrors" too.

Having exhausted all possibilities of finding more George Eliot books in the house library, I peeked in on Norm who was busy at work in his office upstairs. "I'm going to the barn to peruse some books in the loft, dear."

"Be careful of those stairs! I have boxes of books to be shelved on the landing. And the flashlight has moved. It's now hanging at the handrail near the light switch. Look on the right side for George Eliot books. If we have any, that's where they'd be. And...."

As Norm's voice trailed off, I closed the kitchen door behind me and made my way to the barn. The charming antiquated book loft had once been a focal point of our B & B, but slowly it turned into a storage space, a stray cat pad, and a place for my husband to escape the attention of the world. The dust in the barn was enough to send me into wheezing fits. But there were days when I would find my husband sleeping in one of the chairs the cats would claim come nightfall. Surrounded by his books, he seemed the great chronicler—the keeper of the books of life. Dust, cat hair, the lingering odor of chickens from a decades-old coop—nothing seemed to bother him. My husband was much like Robert Evans, a humble, managerial type—a provider of wonderful opportunities for me to expand my understanding of the world.

I could imagine Mary Ann near a window of the Griff barn hayloft, reading a book that excited her to talk straight through supper, and perhaps through family time around the fireplace at night. That was one aspect of Mary Ann's life to which I could not relate. My family had not been the kind to gather together around anything except the dinner table and television. On occasion, we would work together to plant fields or harvest crops. And on very special occasions, my father would sit and tell stories of his childhood: the good old days when he walked barefoot to school and was responsible for starting a fire in the one room schoolhouse stove. But when my books came out, or I would dare request a reading of one of my stories, my family scattered. Looking back on it, my early stories were dreadful.

There were no Eliot offerings in the barn book loft, which by the way looked eerily similar to the Astley Book Farm that housed an enviable George Eliot collection in Warwickshire. I'd found a picture of it during a mad search for Eliot references on the Internet. Someday, I thought to myself, I would sit in the Astley Book Farm sipping stout British tea and perusing the George Eliot collection.

Norm was too busy for a day of book sleuthing, so I kissed him goodbye and drove south to old book haunts near Columbus with the intention of finding the perfect Eliot biography. The Village Bookstore, an old Methodist church converted for the purpose of selling overstocked, out-of-print, and used books, seemed the perfect place to go first. Somehow, it had George Eliot, or at least young Mary Ann

Evans written all over it! And besides, La Chatelaine French Bistro was just up the street with its robust French roast coffee and delectable Napoleons.

Like Lucy entering the wardrobe into Narnia, I made my way through the narrow entrance where once hung a plaque to announce the number who had attended Sunday School each week, where bulletins had lain announcing 101 prayer requests to fend off the toothache, water weight gain, gout, pout, ungrateful kin, and the Pastor's requests for more money for a new church wing (which would never be built). Gone was the alms box, the stack of thumbed-over copies of daily Bible devotion guides. Gone was the smiling Elder in the vestibule with ill-fitting false teeth and the combed-over the bald spot hairdo.

Only the structure of the church remained. Inside, the pews had been replaced by old library tables, cheap swivel chairs of chintzy green velour, and a million and one unusual books organized in a modified Dewey Decimal Classification system. There seemed no rhyme or reason to some of the book placements, especially in the center of the ample rooms. But that was part of its charm. The huge oak tables groaned under the weight of stacked coffee table books— anything from the *Dissect a Frog* book with cellophane fold-outs of entrails to a choice book on Shakespeare that weighed enough to be used for a doorstop and was thick enough to be used for a step stool.

The cashier greeted me in a frumpy beige sweater. A button had gone missing, and some fraying of thread was evident. Her otherwise fashionable appearance told me this sweater was a comfortable old "friend" she wore while standing at the register near the entrance. She adjusted the sweater around her hips, perched on a stool, and began to read a paperback book which was creased with wear. I began to create an Eliot character in my head. Who would the cashier have been: Dorothea of *Middlemarch* perhaps?

I was on top of the world—a chipmunk with a secret stash of acorns. I could tell no one about the Eliot orb discovery except our closest family and friends and Dr. Heinemann, at least not until I had done adequate research on George Eliot. I had to know much more to make my case. To stumble around in the literary darkness with several chapters short of a real book would be unforgivable to an inquiring public. My intentions were out there; I just had to find the right Eliot biography!

The acrid smell of burnt coffee came from an old Mr. Coffee pot sitting near the front desk. Eliot would have been looking for a pot of fresh British blend tea! Soon enough, I escaped into the second room where the literature and religion books were strange bedfellows on connecting shelves. My eyes made a mad sweep for the surnames of authors beginning with E: Eastermann. Edwards: Eggers. ELIOT! There were three Eliot books! One was a modern Signet Classic version of *Silas Marner*. And another *Silas Marner* with a worn cover. And one paperback Oxford edition, *Eliot: Selected Critical Writings*. Not exactly what I wanted, but I pulled the latter one down to have a look and immediately replaced it. Changing my mind, I reached for it again. It might offer something. I sorted through the books on that shelf again. As if by magic, there it was: Thames and Hudson's *Literary Lives: George Eliot* by Marghanita Laski! It looked rich and proper on the shelf—a soft yellow—like Jersey cream. Gingerly I stepped toward one of the velour swivel chairs, dropped into the bucket style seat, and savored the gem in a far corner away from uninvited eyes.

I could fully imagine Eliot's thin piano fingers making their way through the book with haste. Would Eliot approve? I think so! It was packed with illustrations of Eliot's England: the ivy-covered Griff House, family, friends, George Eliot, and her famous soulmate, George Lewes. It was as though the Universe had beaten me to the bookstore and created on that shelf the very book I needed most. Also inside the book was an old painting of Goethe's palatial residence in Weimar, a sketch of the Pariser Platz in Berlin, and a letter from George Eliot to Charles Bray dated 12 November 1854. According to Laski, Charles Bray had been the one who introduced young Mary Ann to philosophical "high thinking." They remained friends for life. As was typical of their relationship, Mary Ann shared a confidence in a letter to Mr. Bray about her new friend, George Lewes, in whom she had found a favorable and lasting companionship: "I think it is impossible for two human beings to be more happy with each other...."

My heart raced as I read through the first several pages of Laski's biography. I was poring over passages that could have been penned by my own hand. And further, my husband was a type of George Lewes, a philosophical companion with whom I shared a quiet, intellectual life, contented with simple comforts found in each other's company.

I tucked the book under my arm as though hiding a treasure, and retraced my steps back to the cash register where the cashier pulled back the book cover beyond my comfort level to check the price. She inquired if I was doing a research paper for college. If I had said yes, she would have let the conversation drop, and I could have been on my way through the vestibule, but *no*, I had to be honest. I told her I was beyond term papers and was just interested in George Eliot. At which time she shared that there hadn't been much interest in George Eliot since she'd been there. She was not a Dorothea. I made haste from the counter as soon as she extended the receipt. She lowered her glasses to follow me as I departed.

If I had lingered another moment, she would have extracted the full story from me. She must have worked for one of those sensational tabloids. She could have reduced me to a fool standing in the vestibule like some sinner who dared to enter church only to become a frozen example of what not to do during an altar call. *How George Eliot was that thought?*

I breathed a deep breath of relief in her absence, lifted the brown bag to my chest, held on tightly, and walked through the vestibule door to the outside world of sanity. *But was there sanity out there? Was I the same woman who walked into the literary dimensional doorway just one hour before?* Then the humorous thought occurred to me that if George Eliot were watching me at that very moment, she would be laughing a genuine belly laugh. I wondered how many times, in the midst of her "holy war" with her father, she had evaded questions and tiptoed past him with a philosophical treasure book hidden under her apron? Duty to self is *not* selfishness. We all had much to learn!

−4−

Karmic Parallels

There was so much to experience, to hope for, and as a woman who was not savoring middle age, the prospect of something fresh, bright, and colorful made my inner child shout with joy. Mystery and adventure were just ahead!

I sent Dr. Heinemann my growing list of parallels between the author, George Eliot, and me. Within hours, he replied to my correspondence, sharing that he thought my parallels list was "outright astonishing!" I was grateful that he was able to make use of my orb photos and information, but my true work in deciphering the Eliot enigma was still ahead of me. I wondered what it meant for my life and for modern readers of Eliot.

Driving myself forward in the quest to learn about Eliot's intrusion on my life, I soon found that I was relying on Dr. Heinemann in much the same way Mary Ann (Eliot) had relied on Charles Bray who introduced her to new ways of thinking about the world. The more I read, the more it seemed that I was living a parallel life with Eliot. There were too many similarities to deny some kind of karmic connection. I don't profess to be Eliot's intellectual equal, or to be a great writer. Far from it! I have always wondered if my writing was worthy. But George Eliot felt the same way: always wondering if she'd done her best—if her writing would be acceptable to her reading public. From my research, I surmised that Eliot was a type A personality, a perfectionist who required much of herself. She would borrow many books at one time, attempting to read them all. If she failed in her endeavor, she would express her guilt in letters to her friends regretting that she had not taken a few extra moments of time to finish reading just one more book.

Laski's biography shared a story of a borrowed book and Mary Ann's intention to commit it to memory. Her sister, Chrissy, was loaned Sir Walter Scott's *Waverly* novel. The seven year old Mary Ann borrowed it from her, but before she could finish reading, Chrissy returned the volume to its owner. Dismayed, Mary Ann began rewriting the book as she remembered it. Sympathizing with Mary Ann, the family retrieved the *Waverly* volume for her to finish. Mary Ann would refer to Scott's novels again and again during her lifetime. She spent most of her early life reading Scott novels to her father, especially when he was bedridden with kidney disease. It must have been a great comfort for Robert Evans to have a daughter that was so considerate of his needs.

Reading literature, science, and philosophy filled Mary Ann's mind with wonder and made her memory rich with prospects for novel writing. But reading was not the only thing that satisfied her desire for culture. She loved music. She played the piano for anyone who would listen: her family, friends, and even hired help. Each performance was fretted over as though she were on the stage in a concert hall. Young Mary Ann was so sensitive about her performance that she would sometimes break into tears and make herself ill. At other times, she appeared to be having a mystical experience while listening to music.

I knew that feeling well. Pachelbel's Canon in D Major, Rhapsody on a Theme of Paganini, Musetta's Waltz, Nessun Dorma, O Mio Babbino Caro, and so many other classical pieces captivated me like a bee to sugary lemonade. I played an electric organ when I was young. I would practice for hours on end, asking anyone who would listen to critique my performance. When they walked away, and would no longer listen, I wept and played behind closed doors. It sounded good enough to me, so I kept right on playing. When I think back on that period, it must have sounded morbid with that droning organ music sounding through our farmhouse year round. But could it be any worse than the depressing country music that played non-stop from the TV and record player console in our living room? Years later, my stepmother told me that she heard that organ long after I left it behind in our childhood home. It was her way of saying that my playing had driven her crazy. As an adult, I made efforts to create improvisational tunes on our mahogany baby grand piano, but I'm certain that the mature and accomplished George Eliot played on her mahogany grand piano in precise concert style.

As children, Mary Ann and I revealed sensitive, artistic natures. But we both had friends around us that would bring out the best we had to offer. Eliot had Miss Lewis, the loving governess she met in 1828 at Mrs. Wallington's Boarding School in Nuneaton, who kept contact with her for life. And later she became best of friends with Cara Bray and Sara Hennell, writing many letters to them over her lifetime. Young Mary Ann was drawn to mature conversationalists and intellectuals. I spent my childhood and young adulthood making friends of older ladies in our neighborhood. I would walk to their homes across a clover field, or make my way down a dusty side road to visit over tea, learn some sewing tips, or sell the ladies of the household something that I carried for miles in a satchel. Mary Ann and I had few friends as children, but those we had were answers to inward prayers.

Mary Ann was also close to her mother, though Isaac was her favorite among the siblings. When Christiana died, it left a huge space in fifteen-year-old Mary Ann's life. It is difficult to understand unless one has experienced such a dramatic life-changing experience. I do understand what Mary Ann went through. She and I were stars without a sky, artwork on an unseen canvas, lyrics without music because the mother who sees, acknowledges, and fosters such talent is missing. The feelings of abandonment are something that can only be eased with the enduring attention of a trustworthy lifelong companion. Mary Ann, as we say in the modern world, had to put on her "big girl panties." She would make several attempts to fill that emptiness, but to no avail until George Henry Lewes became her companion many years later.

I read somewhere that many of the world's enlightened beings lost mothers early. Perhaps it had something to do with the fact that those who were motherless had to struggle to overcome. Buddha's mother died when he was one week old. Though he was spoiled by royal entrapments, he realized something was missing. He was searching for truth--an understanding of the real world. Once outside the palace gates, he saw that others suffered, and that he had been living in a land of make believe. He searched until he learned that he must accept such suffering as part of the human condition. Enlightenment comes to those who embrace truth. We all suffer. As a youngster, I could, for the most part, quell my pain and live a fairly normal life with the help of a few close friends and loyal pet who seemed as though they were spiritually enlightened beings in fur.

One of those loyal pets was Sandy, a beautiful German Shepherd dog that had been given to us because the owner claimed she was mean, but the truth revealed itself in her firm rounded belly—she was pregnant. We learned quickly that German Shepherds are one master dogs. Sandy decided that master was me, and my brothers and friends found it difficult to come near me to play. Sandy lay at the foot of my bed every night. She kept my feet warm during cold farmhouse winters. I felt comforted by her presence. At times, though, I was desperate to know my family loved me. The word love was not spoken in our home. Hugs were not given, and positive feelings were not encouraged.

Then came writing! I could create my own world in my stories. It was a passion that would stay with me for life, and yet another thing I shared in common with Mary Ann Evans. My first publication was poetry in a newspaper at age twenty two. Mary Ann's first publication was a poem in a newspaper at age twenty.

If I had been a human twin to Mary Ann Evans, we would have shared many similarities including likes and dislikes and general personality traits. Except for her long nose, puffy eyes (probably from staying up late to read and write), a prominent chin, and petite figure, there were few physical resemblances between us. I have very dark eyes and dark skin like the character Maggie which Eliot created as her autobiographical match for *The Mill on the Floss*. More importantly, Eliot and I shared many of the same feelings about home and family. Though she was a writer and an intellectual, she believed that women should keep an orderly home and care for their loved ones personally as much as they are able. She enjoyed sewing and had a lovely wood sewing box that she kept during her lifetime.

Young Mary Ann learned from her mother how to cook. She spent long hours in the kitchen preparing foods for her father after her mother died. Gathering currants on the Griff House property was a pleasurable undertaking. However, she was not so fond of cooking the translucent berries to make jelly. The baking of mincemeat pies defined the Michaelmas harvest season. In her early adult letters to friends, she mentioned baking mince pies for her father and for visitors at Christmas.

Mary Ann's mother would have also taught her how to make butter from fresh dairy cream. Mathilde Blind, while doing research for her book, *George Eliot*, interviewed a friend of Mary Ann's who had known her from her Foleshill, Coventry days. The friend said that Mary Ann had shown her that one of her hands was larger than the other. Miss Evans told her friend that it was caused by the quantity of butter and cheese making she had done at the Griff House. In addition, Charles Olcott, author of *George Eliot: Scenes and*

People In Her Novels, mentions this account in relation to Adam Bede and Mrs. Poyser's Dairy, saying she claimed her right hand was larger than her left from working in the dairy. In *Adam Bede*, George Eliot wrote about Mrs. Poyser's Dairy in such detail that it was obvious she'd had some experience in a dairy. Eliot's brother, Isaac, denied his sister's story about making butter, but he denied much of what his sister said and stood for after their separation. I felt this as my own pain.

Like Mary Ann, I gathered berries for jams and pies as a young girl. I ate most of them on the way home from berrying. I remember making my first apple pie when my father showed me how to repair a broken crust. During the Christmas season, I perform traditional kitchen duties, making mincemeat cookies and creating suet pudding from an old English recipe using a pint of Stout and my homemade brandy. As for making butter, we had a Jersey cow on our farm that gave rich cream, so we always had plenty of homemade butter. I was in charge of churning the cream until it solidified around the paddles. Then the butter was shaped into a soft form and chilled. Coincidentally, the knuckles on my right hand are worn, not only from butter-making, but from doing various farm chores as a youth. I'm sure that writing book manuscripts by hand left its mark too.

I remember making clothing for myself as early as fourteen years old. I would take old clothes apart and create patterns for new ones. On occasion, my parents would buy new material so that I could make a nightgown, skirt, or dress. I was mesmerized when I first saw a photo of the George Eliot statue in Nuneaton Square. The dress she wore resembled a dress I had owned. It had a large square Pilgrim collar edged in lace. I also owned a blouse with the same large collar featuring delicate embroidered trim. I do admit it is unusual for someone in this day and age to adore such feminine, old fashioned clothing, but I do. Some kind of karmic kitsch, I guess. When I have a spell for them, I make a mad dash to vintage shops to add pieces to my wardrobe. But then there's the rough and tumble tomboy side of me who loves pants, oversized shirts, and leather boots—Amelia Earhart style!

I believe I am more like young Mary Ann in everyday matters, but I am, in occupation and devotion to accomplishment, inclined toward the writer, Eliot. I could be a twin to the high-spirited character, Maggie, from *The Mill on the Floss*. Since this book is an autobiographical account, it makes sense that I feel like a triptych of persons: Eliot, the author; Mary Ann of Griff; and Maggie, her autobiographical character. Quietly and humbly, I requested Eliot's permission to keep some things she'd passed along to me in this life. My thoughts and written words seem to form as though dropped from another realm. Some would call it channeling—a blend of her intellect and my words. Sometimes I'd awaken with a full page of seemingly dictated prose or poetry! I never knew when the muse of Eliot would move, or when G.O.D. (the Grand Order of Design) would offer revelation about the mysterious universe that aligned Eliot and me. It would seem that karma is a matter-of-fact thing: a rubber stamp that finds a blank sheet on which to imprint itself—the screenplay of the soul. Were the scenes of my soul moving ever forward, creating depth with each succeeding life's rendering—like some mad cartoonist flipping overlays? *Was karma the master artist animating my world?*

I clutched the Laski *George Eliot* biography to me everywhere I went. Perhaps the law of attraction was at work. The more I read, the more believable this karmic imprint seemed! According to the author, it was in Coventry in 1848 that Mary Ann would meet Ralph Waldo Emerson while he was on a lecture circuit in England. She thought him the "the first *man* I have ever seen." And Emerson said of Eliot, "That young lady has a calm, serious soul." The group of writers and intellectuals, including Mary Ann, attended a meeting at Bray's home, Rosehill, followed by a carriage ride to Stratford to enjoy a Shakespeare play. That evening with Emerson was to be one of the highlights of Eliot's life.

I read an archived article, "Ralph Waldo Emerson," in the March 2013 edition of the *Boston Athenaeum*. In the article, Chloe Morse-Harding revealed some of the books that Emerson borrowed from the Boston library during his lifetime. Among the authors were: Moore, Dryden, Holmes, Goethe, and his "...calm, serious..." friend he'd met in England. Ralph Waldo Emerson read books written by George Eliot! It seems they had formed a mutual admiration society. *Could it be that I was drawn to Emerson from an early age by a past life energy imprint associated with Emerson?*

When I was young, I consumed the writings of Ralph Waldo Emerson and Henry David Thoreau. I emulated them by keeping journals about what I'd seen on my walks in the local woods. Nature became a part of me. I *was* nature. I felt God in a direct way by racing through the ferns or standing close enough to feel the spray of a waterfall. My wildness, like Maggie's as she was drawn to the Red Deeps (canals near the Griff House) to join the gypsies, was the beginning of my story and poetry writing. I would have fit in perfectly as a Transcendentalist in the nineteenth century.

I think George Eliot was a Transcendentalist at heart. She embraced many of the "new thinkers" in America—those who initiated and promoted the American Renaissance (from approximately 1835-1880) in literature, poetry, art, music, and architecture (see PBS.org: *Thomas Hampson I Hear America Singing: The American Renaissance & Transcendentalism*). As editor of the Westminster Review in London, Marian (Mary Ann's first pseudonym) wrote a review on Henry David Thoreau's *Walden,* one of my favorite books. Among other movers and shakers in America, was Harriet Beecher Stowe (author of *Uncle Tom's Cabin*). As an adult, I toured the Stowe home in Cincinnati, Ohio. George Eliot had been invited to Stowe's home, but Eliot was unable to make the trip to America. Stowe and Eliot kept regular correspondence through letters which reveal much about their ideals. They were both reformers and teachers through their novels.

I found no evidence that Eliot shared correspondence with Emily Dickinson. However, I recently took my fourth tour of the Dickinson homestead, and there in Emily's bedroom was a picture of George Eliot on the wall facing the street which stretched into Amherst. The moment was so surreal that I almost needed smelling salts to stay on my feet! When I asked the knowledgeable tour guide about the authenticity of the room setting and wall hangings, I was told that they had just redecorated the rooms, and repainted the house to make it more authentic, using paint and wallpaper scrapings and photos of the actual house in which Emily Dickinson had lived. On earlier tours, I had not seen the

George Eliot picture. Apparently Emily *was* aware of George Eliot and admired her work.

Because Ralph Waldo Emerson was the leader of the American Transcendentalists, I visited the Emerson homestead in Concord often. While on vacation, I'd turn up several times in a day during tour hours to ask questions and immerse myself in, what seemed to me, residual wisdom. I could swear it seeped from the woodwork! Emerson's study was a place of sacred reflection. I could almost feel him standing at the bookcase, running a thin finger along a row of leather books, or sitting at his desk with his head bent over an essay that was being written to wake up the world. He would be wearing a dark suit that was easily softened by his gracious smile and soft, fatherly features.

Many of the Transcendentalists spent time at the Old Manse, a lovely country home near the North Bridge where the first shot was to have been fired initiating the American Revolution. It was another surreal moment for me as Norm and I toured the house, grounds, and surrounding area. The Manse was just 300 yards from the North Bridge where the skirmish between the British and the Minutemen took place. At the time of the battle, Emerson's Grandfather owned the home. Ralph Waldo Emerson would later write a poem, *Concord Hymn*, describing the scene as related by his grandfather.

In the backyard of the Manse, was a huge elongated boulder on which the Concord philosophers and writers would sit to discuss deep matters. I found myself lingering there, hoping to absorb the wisdom energy of Ralph Waldo Emerson, Henry David Thoreau, Amos Bronson Alcott, and other Concord contemporaries. Nathaniel Hawthorne and his wife, Sophia, whose sister, Elizabeth Peabody, was a Transcendentalist, rented the old Manse for a time. The Hawthorne's etchings appear on the original window panes where they recorded for perpetuity their affectionate sentiments with Sophia Hawthorne's diamond ring. Talk about a moment etched in time!

On the outskirts of Concord, Emerson's huge granite monument in Sleepy Hollow Cemetery stands in stark juxtaposition to Thoreau's small white stone which is the size of a loaf of bread and contains only his first name, "Henry." I knelt near the stone and wept. He was buried in a family plot on Author's Ridge in the same cemetery, each member with a corresponding stone with first name only. In the center was a Thoreau family marker. The markers were fitting for each of the philosophers: Emerson's larger-than-life image in the world, and Thoreau's humble ways rooted locally in nature. The two men, together with other new thought leaders such as Bronson Alcott (father of Louisa May) borrowed from the sacred Eastern text, the Bhagavad Gita, to help form the ideas that were to transform the thinking of the world.

George Eliot and I both drew strength from these dynamic figures and their philosophy of Transcendentalism.

Though Mary Ann waved the banner of Christianity through her twentieth year, when she met Charles Bray and other "new thinkers" after moving to Coventry, she laid that banner down and picked up another: the belief that the primary focus should be on humans and their worth as divine creatures, not their lack of worth and sinfulness. She had embraced liberal theology. Mary Ann, for the first time in her life, refused to go to church with her father. She considered moving out when her father threatened to leave her at the Foleshill house and move in with another family member. Then came the softening of wills. Mary Ann and her father agreed that she should stay at Foleshill, and her church attendance would continue even if she no longer believed what the church taught. And so it was.

Robert Evans took seriously his honorable standing in the community, and in fact was a "sidesman" or usher at Holy Trinity Church in Coventry. Here we find the outward compromise of Mary Ann, while inwardly she banked the coals of her desire for the sake of a dear relationship. She would find herself in compromising positions many times in her life, eventually writing the circumstances into the plots of her novels. Her readers never quite knew which came first: the real life scene or the fictional one. The author had much to draw on from real life. The provincials thought Mary Ann's actions nothing less than scandalous. Still, Mary Ann was practicing tolerance of others and their ideas. It would serve her well in years to come. The times were changing, and she was changing with them. Her writing was to become the oasis in the desert of rigid English values. Time for tea— strong tea!

–5–

Friends Forever

In the cheesy autograph books of youth, we had pet names for one another. Cuteness and sarcasm were required. I was known as Fred, FeFe, and Skeeter to name a few. "Fred" because I was a tomboy; "FeFe" because my hair was naturally curly like that of a French Poodle; "Skeeter" because I was all arms and legs! Rarely did anyone call me Freda except my teachers, and my stepmother and father. My parents would add my middle name for emphasis when *you-know-what* was about to hit the fan! My childhood friends still call me by various pet names.

George Eliot used several names, and there were a few more names given her by literary critics like Thomas Carlyle and Henry James. They could be downright cruel. Knick names are how others see us. Pseudonyms are how the creative people see the multi-faceted versions of themselves. I used a pen name many years ago, until Norm, the pragmatist, said, "Why would you use a pen name if you want people to know you by your work?" That hit me squarely in my author's ego. I dropped the pseudonym!

I have old friends with whom I correspond regularly. These comfortable relationships came to me in childhood when I leaned on neighbor ladies with their laps full of sewing, or the neighborhood fellows who sat on crates of cream soda at Poole's store jawing their tobacco. They had stout names like Elmer, Frank, and Manuel. This kind of personal communication was typical for the little Upper Midwest towns where I grew up. Of all of my childhood acquaintances, a few stood out. One wrote Tarzan stories at a young age. Another created plays for our cafeteria stage in elementary school. Still another carried a 4.0 average like an easy badge right through high school. His mother was an artist. I liked that! He spent recess creating pictures of distant places: sandy beaches and palm trees laden with coconuts. It was one of my first impressions of how it might feel to travel.

As I began to emerge from my crablike shell of childhood, I formed new friendships similar to Mary Ann's bond with the Brays, the "free thinking" oddballs of Coventry. At the center of their relationship were books—lots of books with new and interesting topics. How could Mary Ann resist? She and I had that in common too. Yes, I kept company with those who were considered creative thinkers. Some of them were just downright brilliant. Most of our correspondence was limited to seasonal school days. Though summer correspondence was rare, the friendships were timeless—

surreal like those few intense beams of sunlight that sneak through the clouds on an overcast day. There was no telephone in our home to keep us informed. It had long since been disconnected for non-payment when my older brother joined the Army and the two-way calls ran up the bill. I think of the modern methods of correspondence by cell phones, emails, and social sites, and I have to wonder if my friends and I would have remained steady through such habitual connections. Back then, we believed that absence made the heart grow fonder. We had to work hard at communication and friendship as a whole. If my stepmother permitted me to stay with a friend for the weekend, we more than made up for lost time, chatting like "Cathy" dolls. My new friends, the Heinemanns, were karmic friends, ones who appeared when the energy was right for them. They came like spirit guides and imparted wisdom. They were in the background of my life with two addresses somewhere in California and a casa in Brazil.

George Eliot was a master at the art of correspondence, both verbal and written. Proper communication was the most important aspect of her being. During her lifetime, she wrote a plethora of letters in long hand, posting them from England and the Continent (Europe) to friends, family, and professional acquaintances. She desired to be understood and to understand others because she knew this was the secret door to empathy between correspondents. Her joy of communicating turned to agony when she moved in with her soulmate, George Lewes. Her family sent letters of rejection. Her brother, Isaac, was successful at turning the whole family away in bitter judgment of his sister's behavior in London. I'm sure Mary Ann (now calling herself Marian and Mrs. Lewes) wept bitter tears, but she stood her ground. She weathered the rejections with steadfast correspondence from friends who were as open-minded as she.

As I gathered facts about George Eliot's life, I added more parallels to my list when they were too similar to ignore. The Heinemanns decided to include nearly a dozen of these with *The Mill on the Floss* project story to be published in their *Orbs* book. In May 2009, Dr. Heinemann wrote to say that they were 20,000 words into their book, which would include approximately ninety of their best orb photos from around the world. He always added that he and Gundi were looking forward to reading my book.

The book to which Dr. Heinemann referred was his visionary hope for the full account of my story. He encouraged me to include our joint work, *The Mill on the Floss* research project, together with research I would conduct on my own and with the help of other good friends such as my AIHT (American Institute of Holistic Theology) advisor, Annette. She and I were similar souls. She'd lost her mother when she was young, so she could understand my pain of being a motherless daughter. Annette was a heroine of mine. She traveled to India, learned to play the sitar and to belly dance. There she made friends with an Indian woman who became her spiritual mom. In her spare time, she created a traveling labyrinth and carried it from place to place, providing an instant sacred experience for those fortunate to find her in their midst. Traveling to Haiti, she assisted with the care and schooling of children whose families had been victims of the devastating earthquake of 2010 that took an estimated 250,000 lives.

Had Annette lived in the Victorian period, George Eliot would have acknowledged her as one of the "new thinkers," a woman who stood for the empathy and love the world so much needed. She was a model of Dorothea in *Middlemarch*. But Annette lived a modern life similar to the protagonist, Liz, in the book *Eat, Pray, Love*. She was always busy, but had time for everyone. Annette was helpful, setting up a time to review some of my research photos I sent to her for evaluation and comment. Gaining the agreement of her monthly psychic share group, she was sending emails with photo attachments to get numerous responses for my research project. I submitted my best orb photos without telling them the subject matter, or where the photos were taken. I *did* ask them to concentrate on any areas that seemed to be brighter than others in the photos. Among these unique photos was the original of *The Mill on the Floss* orb photo which I'd sent to Dr. Heinemann.

The responses were intriguing! One person in particular said that she felt there was a secret room behind the library wall in our home just from viewing a photo. She also said there appeared to be a "black hole" in that same photo. Little did the responder know that a room had been added behind the east library wall. That wall originally had a doorway which was now covered and supporting bookcases. Behind that same wall was a large black Jacuzzi tub—a whirlpool bath—the black hole! I was amazed at how much this participant was able to ascertain from a simple photo. Clearly she had psychic abilities.

In another photo, many of the psychic share members identified the same characteristics of orbs as pets. Another playful orb perched on the seat of a bicycle planter, they identified as a child. I had felt the same responses myself to that photo. Still another photo revealed a curved arch of light rising from a chair on our patio. The majority responded that this was a vortex, and one added that there was probably a water dome underneath the patio—that something special may have happened there before the patio was poured. Our property is situated over an aquifer, and is surrounded by ponds, wetlands, vernal pools, and streams. In the process of researching water domes and ley lines, I learned that the energy acted in odd ways over Southern England near Stonehenge and Avebury, offering up frequent anomalies. The abundant presence of orbs in photos were beginning to make sense to me. I knew there were ley lines in Ohio, and many sacred sites such as Native American burial mounds.

I shared my findings of the psychic study with Dr. Heinemann. We began to communicate on a first name basis through dozens of email exchanges sharing thoughts about orbs, and in particular the growing number of parallels between Eliot's life and my own. No one was more shocked than I about the number of similarities, let alone the fact that the search had initiated with an orb in a photograph. Dr. Heinemann explained that the orbs were consciousness, and that in his new book they were sharing photos that exhibited proof that the orbs were interacting with them and others as the photos were being taken. I was thankful that I had contacted Dr. Heinemann. I had learned so much from him already.

Over the summer months of 2009, the Heinemanns shared detailed information about their forthcoming book. My husband wondered when I put my own book on hold, and began to edit the Heinemann's manuscript. He warned, "You need to concentrate on your own work, dear, or you will just continue spinning in space every time someone needs help." But I needed the experience of reading and editing. I would plant a seed and watch it grow over my fence to drop seeds for future prosperity. Good karma!

The documentation for the Heinemann's new book was extremely thorough. They had traveled the world in search of quality orb photos, and I was proud to be one of their contributors. While editing, I tried to absorb what the Heinemanns were saying to their readers. I had seen many orbs in photographs: around children playing, in areas where nature was unspoiled, where a sense of peace was pervasive, and where joy was present. Even though I photographed orbs, and had sensed something was obviously "personal" about them, I had not yet seen the true relevance of these amazing glowing energy forms. With my own Eliot experience, I had only begun to open a door that Klaus and Gundi had opened years ago. And yet, somehow, my compelling story was integral to the value of their new book.

Editing with care, I worked day and night to complete the task within a week. It occurred to me that I was imitating Eliot—editing for a friend—just as she had done for John Chapman, owner of the *Westminster Review.* I was filled with awe that somehow the Universe had brought the Heinemanns together with me to lend credence to the Eliot epiphanies. My friends were grateful for the editing I'd done on their book, and as a thank you, they sent me two of Dr.

Heinemann's books: *Consciousness and Entropy* and *Expanding Perception.*

For now, my work of editing the Heinemann's book was done. It was time for me to move forward—to research a possible parallel life I seemed to be having with George Eliot. I wondered what the modern world would make of George Eliot—if she would be a friend they could believe in— someone with whom they could confide their deepest wishes and dreams. Her love of correspondence was ingrained in her spirit personality, so I had no doubt she would produce some soul-satisfying impressions, if not direct revelations.

Freda M. Chaney

–6–

Mirrored Moments

Much in life depends on permission from family, peers, culture, politics, and religion. To overcome the need of others' strict authority over us, we have to grant ourselves permission to be individuals first. I individuated early! The Transcendentalists had done their work in me. I was living what I believed.

George Eliot also lived what she believed. She was different, and she knew it. She spoke purposefully and powerfully through her novels to cut a path of human equality through the oak groves of Arden, to the soft pine forests of the Continent (Europe), all the way to the stands of locust in young America. Eliot, the writer, stood tall and strong like those native Warwickshire oaks, her presence spreading branches over the landscape of the world.

In an article titled, *"Mr. and Mrs. Cross with the artist John Wharlton Bunney,"* by Sarah Bunney in the March 2012 issue of *The George Eliot Review*, I learned of Eliot's strong desire to see the "Madonna of Mercy" triptych, created by Bartolomeo Vivarini, at the altar of Santa Maria Formosa Church in Italy. She admired the center panel that was of the Madonna sheltering saints (perhaps parishioners) within her robe. Eliot's moral beliefs were a depiction of that scene. I believe she identified herself in that painting as a "voice" of equality—of human decency that spoke out for those who had no voice of their own. Eliot eventually did see the original triptych in Venice in 1880 while on honeymoon with John Walter Cross. I can imagine her there, eyes aglow with wonder, gloved hands clasped together at her waistline, lost for words, simply experiencing the reverence of the moment.

The being that was I—who had dominated my life for as long as I could remember—knew well this "Eliot affirmation" of human equality and its resulting empathy. I felt I needed to share with anyone who would listen. That desire would design my life for me—would lead me to places of solitude for thinking and writing. My little office over the stairs, the maid's quarters of the original homestead, was the perfect haven for structuring the Eliot affirmation of the soul in my own words for modern readers.

Clamped between two large dutiful bookends, my collection of George Eliot books grew. Some were newer editions; some were vintage hardcovers with uneven yellowed pages, broken spines, and frayed ribbon markers.

Looking at the collection made me realize what an important writer George Eliot was then and now. Queen Victoria's reign brought about a change in social mores. Under her watch, the Romantic Period bloomed. Queen Victoria was, in fact, born in the same year as George Eliot, 1819, and according to Marghanita Laski's research, the Queen admired Eliot's writings, and even commissioned paintings of famous scenes in her novels.

The recognition and respect that George Eliot sought from her family and society was not to be had, but she could take pride in her work, and find acceptance among some of England's best. Her books struck a match of admiration among the Transcendentalists in America as well. Even children enjoyed Eliot's writing and sent letters to her. She responded to each and every one, taking special care with her responses to children. Communication is my forte as well, and I especially love interacting with children. Their responses are genuine.

In these mirrored moments, I could see my entire life rolled out like a dense, heavy carpet leading back to Eliot's own. There would be many such moments when my jaw would drop, my eyes would open wider, and my finger would trace the pages of a book hungrily for additional clues leading me, always, back to myself. Daily rooted in my office to research and write, I listened to the phone ringing-up reservations, black capped chickadees chirping at the window like miniature nuns fussing about an abbey, the decided step of shoes on the worn back stairs. These were my only distractions from Eliot except for Sadie, the cute Pembroke Welsh Corgi that sat at my feet. She was a fur kid to Norm and me.

I wondered how many feet had traveled those stairs during the 200 years after the house was built, and how many different styles of shoes or boots might have landed on each stair wearing depressions into the treads. Perhaps a nanny's charges had pulled sock dolls and corn cob toys over the polished steps, bumping their way to the primitive kitchen below. The nanny might follow behind carrying the chamber pot. Such a house would be bustling with life: hired hands coming and going, mud sticking to the plank board flooring. In the air, the heavenly smell of bacon frying on the monstrous black cook stove would bring the master from the western side of his house. Thick farmhouse coffee would empty quickly from a black graniteware coffeepot and be refilled a dozen times during the day. The cook's heavy hands, tainted with potato and onion juice, would lay two fat brown loaves of wheat bread on the cutting board, slice through them with ease, and lay the thick slices slathered with fresh butter atop the cook stove to keep them warm. It was all so Eliot!

Our Federal style house looks remarkably similar to the Georgian style of the Griff House. The Federal style evolved from the Georgian style popular in Britain in the 1800s. Mary Ann would have been four years old when our house was erected in 1823. She was likely charming the entire household with her imagination at that age.

I was meant for this rural and literary way of life the same way Eliot was meant for her beginnings at Griff. The purity and hard work, nature and its challenges, rising with the rooster and reading by dim light at bedtime—all of these we held in common. There was a deep connection with the country, with its people, with the souls that laced themselves like boots to the landscape. When my husband and I planned our move from the suburbs to a rural manor house, some tried to talk us out of the purchase, fearing it would be too much work for us, and the B & B too involved to allow for family visits and Sunday church. It was rewarding having stood firmly in our independent convictions that our lives were to be lived as we chose now that we were coupled in this literary life together. *And wasn't that just what Eliot and Lewes had done?*

I tried to imagine what George Eliot would be doing on the summer day I was experiencing just then. Would she be at home pushing her pen to write more and more, disobeying a sharp ache in her wrist? Perhaps she'd be strolling on a gray London walkway, stopping to purchase yeast rolls from a street vendor's basket. She might be dining in a blue crinoline-supported dress with pilgrim collar. Would the mysterious lady lean over a bone china teacup and lift the steaming beverage with her ink-stained right hand? Would her soulmate join her on such a day? Not likely. But if he did, and if they could without social ostracism, he would reach to pat her delicately-gloved hand and reassure her of his devotion. The evening of such a day might find the couple at either side of the "snug" (a cozy room with fireplace) like a set of parentheses, her feet set firmly upon the fender for warmth. She might be reading an announcement of a future visit by Emerson, a handbill for a Liszt concert in Berlin, or one last letter from her disagreeable relatives back in the Midlands.

Looking for a tidbit or two to spur my creativity for the day, I pulled Laski's *George Eliot* biography from my desk-top collection and thumbed through it again. The familiar black and white pictures had become like a treasured family photo album to me. Hours later, I pulled myself up from my desk chair having a feeling of lost time. I had been there so long in one position with my eyes riveted on the text, I was unaware that the day had sneaked away.

Who or what was trying to tell me I was so similar that perhaps I was George Eliot reincarnated? It was even more incredible than that—it seemed I was reliving her Victorian life in the modern world: a parallel life! The evidence was mounting daily, and Dr. Heinemann agreed that perhaps a past life reading might answer some questions that were haunting me. But he reinforced the fact that I could take or leave the findings. "A past life is just that, and you needn't relive it if you choose not to do so," Dr. Heinemann said. "Accept what helps you in this life, and discard the rest."

I certainly did not want to relive Eliot's life; my own life had been painful enough! And yet George Eliot was a successful writer in her time, moving beyond the restrictions of the Victorian period to become a classic icon in British literature. *How harmful could such an association be?* Onward then, bringing Eliot into the light of the modern world, juxtaposing her with the modern woman who offered no excuses, gave no ground, and dealt from the top of the deck to anyone who would play. I'd believe for the best.

Freda M. Chaney

–7–

Valley of Decision

M y stepmother used to say that I was stubborn. But it was my willpower that she saw, not stubbornness. I was not one to open and close like the crepe paper Christmas bells she brought out each December and put away in January. I was not easily persuaded. It took philosophical books, strangers with fresh stories from out of town, a movie with the real ring of human existence like Steinbeck's *The Grapes of Wrath*, or a mentor who took the time to guide me toward plausible conclusions. I was small, but my dreams were large. I had to learn to stifle my energy at rare times to save myself from parental wrath. I did not expect them to understand. They were leaners on the land, fetched-up in country traditions. I didn't fit the mold perfectly. I had aspirations for something completely different; something big—bigger than the town that claimed me at birth, bigger than the clan that tried to hold me there like a pushpin to the bulletin board of their lifestyle.

Eliot would certainly have known the feeling of being too big for one's life. She made many choices that none other in her family of record had made. She was strong-willed, independent, followed her instincts, and it served her well. Her sensitive spirit and frail body suffered the consequences, but she honored her individuality and pushed herself to achieve. She tops the list of nineteenth century British female novelists. Some even say that George Eliot's genius compares to that of Shakespeare! Her achievement would not have been possible had young Mary Ann Evans listened to what others had said: go to church, be a good wife, raise a passel of kids. Sounds familiar!

Had George Eliot been born in the 20th century, perhaps she would have joined hands with marching activists in their quests for equal rights for women, and better education for children. She might have been an anti-war, sign carrying hippie in the 1960s, or a "no nukes" Green party member in the 1970s and 1980s. But as it was, Eliot limited her activism to the landscapes of her books. Therein she could draw lines, give speeches, and deliver holy writs all from the characters' own lips. She was a master at keeping an open mind with her characters. Once they were established in the story, if they were evangelical, she allowed them to be so. If they were drunks who spent the last family dime selfishly, then so be it. She allowed the characters to set matters to right within the framework of their own situations. Eliot did not judge within the pages of her books, but preferred realism and hope in looking forward to positive change. That hope, she thought, depended on the passing of time and the belief that people were capable of bettering themselves.

From time to time, I immersed myself in local activism, coordinating activities with an environmental group. Most in our area restricted their concerns to cows and corn. Traditional farmers didn't hug trees or wave banners for animals' rights. But there was a handful who made it their business to protect the land, grow organic crops, and further the cause of preservation in our area. They seemed like "displaced Californians." So I was not the only odd fellow talking to butterflies and creating backyard wildlife habitats. I tried to understand both sides of the story. The farmers needed to survive by growing abundant crops, and that meant using chemicals. Some who could afford it, were using no-till farming methods. This meant injecting weed and insect control along with fertilizer into the same hole where the seed was planted. There was less erosion of the soil with the no till method, but the seed swam in a chemical bath.

Louis Bromfield, a local writer-turned-conservationist, introduced no-till farming to our area, but he used natural fertilizers. Malabar Farm, the home he built in 1939, is less than thirty miles away. It is now known as Malabar Farm State Park. Bromfield wrote fiction (*The Green Bay Tree, The Rains Came, Mrs. Parkington*) and later, non-fiction (*Malabar Farm, Up Ferguson Way*) which brought him much acclaim. He also wrote screen plays for Hollywood where he met and made fast friends with the elites, inviting them to Malabar Farm to experience the serenity of rural Ohio—and the hard work that went with it. Bromfield required guests to choose a chore to cover room and board if they extended their stay. So when Humphrey Bogart and Lauren Bacall got married at Malabar Farm in 1945, they may have been working in the barnyard after a brief honeymoon in the sprawling Greek Revival style house. James Cagney visited Bromfield and worked the Malabar Farm vegetable stand during his stay. I wonder if he wore his fedora hat. I can just hear customers asking him to do a gangster imitation for them. "You're the dirty rat who bagged the beets!" It must have been great fun for the Hollywood elites to step out of their melodramatic screenplay lives and meet their friend, Louis, on a dusty Ohio back road, there to cut loose with simple country humor.

When I think of Bromfield, I can't help but think of Eliot's father, Robert Evans, the self-taught manager of the Newdigate estates in the Midlands of England. Bronson Alcott, the Fruitlands farmer, Utopian dreamer, and Transcendentalist friend of Emerson also comes to mind. Norm and I loved them all! We loved to hear about their agrarian ideas—old fashioned though they were. We once attended a meeting of Luddites in Barnesville, Ohio. I sat on the bleachers taking notes and sketching chubby-cheeked

Amish children and bearded men in patched denim overalls. It seemed the clocks had been turned back one hundred years!

Norm and I loved spending time in the country too. We drove to Port Royal, Kentucky once to see the farm of a famous writer-activist, Wendell Berry. I read a book of his essays to Norm as we snaked our way down through the Appalachian hills. Another time we drove to Massachusetts to see the only circular barn built by the Shakers, the Shaker Round Stone Barn at Hancock Shaker Village. Some confuse the Shakers with the Amish. The Shakers did not believe in marriage and having children. The communities eventually closed doors, and private groups reopened some of them to the public under the protection of the National Historic Landmark District. There had once been nineteen Shaker villages across the U.S.

There are many Amish farmers in our area. They believe in living off the land, and have a strong sense of family and community. Their communities continue to grow across the U.S. They use natural fertilizers from their animals to enrich the soil for growing crops. Norm and I prefer Amish produce when we are unable to grow our own. Juxtapose the scene of an Amish farmer with his team of horses spreading manure onto his freshly cultivated fields, and the crop duster pilot performing daring feats over our Delano Flood Plain, making numerous passes, nearly clipping the tree tops as he closes in to drop huge loads of chemicals. I would watch and weep. *What about the bees and butterflies? Don't they have a right to live? Are we slowly killing ourselves by killing the pollinators?*

The locals were pragmatists who saw nature to be used as God had intended: to serve man. Our fight was not just against pollution caused by poor agricultural practices, but it was against the farmers' God. They had tilled the land for generations. Their sweat had built the town and surrounding countryside. I saw the streambeds being raped of trees, and farm fields being piped. A letter to the E.P.A. would bring someone out to check the site, with a report to follow saying they could do nothing since it was a farmer piping his own fields.

When I put up a protest to say that the run-off would pollute the north fork of our beloved Licking River and beyond, the administrators said, "You have just cited the #2 reason for pollution to waterways: runoff from agricultural activity. There is nothing we can do until they pollute." I wrestled with the lack of logic. *Why allow them to rape the streams, lay the pipe, pollute the waterways, and then cite them for polluting? What ever happened to the idea of prevention?*

Here, on the floodplains, a common sight is the red-tailed hawk sweeping down to pick up field mice in its sharp beak, flying to a territorial perch to stand tall above its catch. Sometimes I felt like one of those helpless mice, wondering what came next if I exposed myself too much in the fields of life. *Had George Eliot felt the same anxiety about her bold friends marching for women's rights?* My life had been a collection of risk-taking ventures. When Norm and I got engaged, we asked the age-old question, "What would people say?" We'd both been married before, there was a great difference in our ages, and our family backgrounds couldn't be more different. One day, we had to turn the volume down on the concerned chatter, and trust our own judgment for a happy ending. Nothing is ever perfect, and as Eliot knew, all things take time. Time was the great healer. Like the farmer who must first plow his field, then disc it, fertilize it, plant the seed, hoe the weeds, watch the weather, pray, and finally harvest the crop, marriage needed time—there were seasons for marriage—just as there were seasons for sowing and reaping.

Most of the winter and spring months I'd spent pondering Eliot, learning who she was, what she had to say to me. I trusted the Heinemanns with my research story, and now I needed to trust the process as it unfolded to reveal the full Eliot mystery. Trust would bring answers. Dr. Heinemann said something in a recent email that stuck with me, "If the soul's blueprint for its lifetime journey is not met during an incarnation, chances are it will need another incarnation to complete the mission." That statement confirmed what he said to me earlier about taking what was important to me and letting the rest go. Each lifetime has its individual value, and it should be lived to its fullest without spending too much time nursing regrets. If I *had* been George Eliot in a past life, I wouldn't want to relive her karmic mistakes in my current life! If the reading had something positive to offer to me that would project me forward—improve my life, then I would keep it, and the rest I would discard as Dr. Heinemann had suggested.

Some members of my family thought it might be detrimental to have a past life regression because I was too young to remember my mother's death. They feared I might witness her passing and experience grief as though it had just happened. When I was nine years old, one of my cousins told me that my mother died as a result of my birth. That comment sent me wailing through the floppy screen door and into the farmhouse kitchen where my aunts and uncles were playing a card game of Rummy 500 with my parents. I was redirected into my parents' bedroom where I fell face down onto their bed. I can still hear my own muffled cries, and smell the acrid coal scent that possessed the hand-stitched quilt on the creaky double bed. My stepmother came from behind telling me to stop crying.

"What on Earth is wrong with you, Freda?" There was no sweet wiping of tears, or hugs to stay off gargantuan, life-changing words. "That's ridiculous!" was her reply after I told her why I was crying. "You were nine months old when she died! Now go wash your face and get back outside and play!" It was her way. Not that I liked it. She just wasn't one to offer warmth. I had caused a scene. Another lost moment between us—another lost chance to bond.

God help me if I had to relive my mother's death only to find that some had spared my feelings by saying I was not responsible. Still, I felt ready to move forward. I'd spent most of my life wondering about my birth, what took place just before my mother's death, why there were no pictures of us together. I needed some answers. Should clues surface while peering into the past for George Eliot, then so be it. Perhaps, at long last, I would have some definitive answers. And no matter what, I'd have Norm's loving support.

Just as George Lewes supported George Eliot, my husband was the support pole in my scarecrow. No matter the little irritations and rare moments of disconnection, we were happy even when we disagreed with one another, and that was something I'd only previously experienced in books and movies with happy endings. We were one, forged from a need to have a significant other with whom to share life's most important moments—both large and small. We had each other's permission to be individuals, and to say "no" when we needed to do so. I was thankful that Norm was in the cheering section for me. While it was true that my husband could do with less Eliot, he was an English professor who was obliged to have me learn what lesson another writer's life had to teach me. He had known me since my college days. Perhaps he wanted some of Eliot's narrative skill to rub off on me, or give me a dose of her courage to move my books into the marketplace and get my voice heard.

Norm was consistent and persistent. He'd spent nearly ten years writing to me after I left college. He charmed my mailbox with Christmas cards, notes, letters, and once he sent a cassette tape of himself singing. I remember his pastoral poems set to music. We were just friends then. Ten years later, I knew he was serious when he asked me to stop in and see him the next time I was in town. One would think there had been a romance between us when I was his student, but not so. He kept his work and his love life separate as far as I knew.

My daughter, Vicki, also supported me in my quest for answers. Vicki could be likened to Sara Hennell, sister of Cara Bray, two of Eliot's dearest friends, both "free thinkers" and loyal supporters of others who were. Vicki and I had practically grown up together. I was only nineteen when she was born. I learned what it meant to have a mother by being a mother to Vicki. I knew no matter what, she would approach my work with an open mind and be there when I needed a sounding board. She thought having a past life regression sounded interesting!

When I studied Reiki for my advanced degree, I learned to relax and allow myself to "see" what healing was necessary for myself and others. I decided to try some deep meditation techniques to fish for Eliot clues. The first session brought forth many images, I slept through the second session, and the third, fourth, and fifth sessions were as productive as the first. When the sessions were over, I hurriedly jotted down notes and drew sketches of what I'd experienced while the images were fresh in my mind.

The major impressions I received from the first session were a dark dress with a tight waist, medical instruments, and an old man with a large nose and closed eyes. Then, suddenly, the scene changed to a mother's eyes, a blanket opening to reveal a baby's face, and gifts as though there was a celebration of birth. In addition I saw a door, and near the door was a dark secretary style desk. I could actually see the grain of the wood. In the third session, I saw a glass of wine, flat shoes flanked by higher heeled shoes, and antique photo frames. In session four, I saw who I assumed to be George

Lewes. He looked much like the self portrait of Rembrandt! He was inside a house standing near a beautiful arched window. There was a winding staircase. Oddly, in the same scene was a placemat or a square of paper that had fern-like patterns on it. I didn't trust my own mind enough to conclude the findings from these deep meditations. I filed the session notes away, and chalked up the "visions" to my unusually active and colorful imagination.

Once I decided to have a professional past life regression, the Hay House book, *Repetitions: Past Lives, Life, and Rebirth* by Doris Cohen, Ph.D. immediately came to my attention. Upon examination of the book, I knew that Dr. Cohen was the next person to whom I would entrust the unfolding of my mysterious connection with George Eliot. In her book, she encouraged readers to rewrite their lives. That appealed to me! I was doing that every day when I awoke to jot down similarities between Eliot and me. I was evolving with each journal entry. I immediately penciled Dr. Cohen into my things-to-do list. I was ready to tell my story to the world, but was the world ready to hear it? "Obscure Ohio writer meets world famous London author in a past life regression session! Coming soon to a literary looney bin near you!" At least I still had a sense of humor.

–8–

Past Life Reading

Sometimes I laughed until I cried, and sometimes I just cried! What was happening to me? My subconscious self was knee-deep in communication with my conscious self. It was a constant two-party line connection that would have made Jung envious. I believe George Eliot had been keenly aware that consciousness was moving in sync with her subconscious mind. She could not have written so explicitly about the deep inner workings of the soul, or how the mind tries to create fantasy when reality cannot provide what is needed to nourish the soul. When she had a need to express her feelings, she created plots, characters, and dialogue to express to the world the ideas she was trying to convey. Writing was therapy for us both. But writing was not enough to ease my anxiety. I needed proof—proof that this Eliot lady had a real connection to me.

I made an appointment with Dr. Doris Cohen and waited for her calendar to clear. She interviewed me briefly, asking what I wanted to gain from the past life reading. Reading? She said it would be easier, less expensive for me, and perhaps bring better results if we had a past life reading over the phone. She pointed out that I could make several trips to her office, go under hypnosis, and still get fewer results than if she connected with her Guides as she conversed with me over the phone. Of course, I decided to have the reading over the phone. When giving Dr. Cohen preliminary information, I was vague on purpose, not allowing any clues to my Eliot findings. I told her I was writing a book about my life, and wanted to include the notes from our session.

"Do I have your permission to include the information from our reading?"

"Of course," she said in a thick accent. "What difference would it make?"

"I just want to be sure you understand that I may be publishing the information I learn from the reading."

"That will be fine. Sure!" she added.

The waiting seemed forever until the day of my reading. During those long weeks, I kept busy doing research, writing, and taking an occasional photograph to be sure I could still see orbs. I saw them as angels of light, offering their benevolence, perhaps temporary benevolence. Who knew for sure? We were all out there creating our own hypotheses about the unknown.

The phone rang on a sunny day in late August, 2009. I picked up the receiver, and Dr. Cohen's happy voice piped through.

"Freda, Doris Cohen here. Are you ready for your past life reading?"

"Hello, Dr. Cohen. Yes, I am very eager to get started."

"Very well. We will begin with a blessing."

I bowed my head and thought about how I'd prepared for this call. I prayed, I meditated, I blessed my room with holy water that a friend had obtained from a Catholic church basin, I read Psalms, I asked my daughter to pray for me, and I thought long and hard about what I would do with the information I learned from the session with Dr. Cohen.

"...Amen. Freda, let's get started now. It will take a few moments for me to go into a trance."

A trance following the blessing? It seemed a bit spooky, but I couldn't back out now! I was in for the duration.

About one minute passed, and then Dr. Cohen began to speak. "You were a black male child on a slave ship in a past life. The children were separated from their mothers, and you and the other children were distraught. Even though you were placed in a good home, and treated well, you never saw your mother again, and you grieved. You lost your voice for many years because of that grief."

There was a pause, and I needed one! I had had dreams about being in the company of young African Americans. I defended one of the girls when a boy bullied her and made her cry. It wasn't a perfect fit, but it was very close. In the dream, the bully started shrinking until he almost disappeared. Finally, he ran away. There is a lesson here already: face your problems and they will flee.

Dr. Cohen resumed, "You were a spiritual male in the age of Nostradamus. You healed people, and the church charged you as a heretic and burned you at the stake. Again, in this life, you lost your voice."

"Most interesting," I interjected. "I am an advanced Reiki practitioner. I have a divinity degree, and pray for people. I certainly fit the template of healer in *this* life. It seems to come naturally to me. Sometimes it seems I am an empath, sensing others' pain."

She didn't miss a beat. "Your wife warned you not to heal people any more. She feared that you would be found out. And your daughter in that life is your grandson now. That grandson is very close to you, yes? So it was with you and your daughter in that life in France. Both of you have a deep intuitive sense and psychic abilities."

At that point, my pencil stopped writing. I was mesmerized by what she was saying. There was clearly a pattern to the lives: separation, grief, loss of voice.

"You were the daughter of a French performer—a singer and stage actress. You were the eldest daughter, and your mother resented you because you took up her time; her heart was at the theater. You were left at home alone, and you grieved for your mother."

Incredible! That had happened in my own life—this life more than once. Not the theater, but the fact that my caretakers left. I wanted to tell Dr. Cohen about my mother's death, my first stepmother leaving, and my second stepmother leaving at least twice. I restrained myself and continued to listen. What she had to say to me was more important than what I had to say to her.

"Let me take a moment here, Freda. Yes, you need to work at getting your voice heard. This book that you are writing should help do that for you."

"Nothing about Eliot," I thought to myself.

"My Spirit Guides are asking what else you want to know."

"Well, I am wondering if I am related to a certain writer...you see, I saw this orb..."

"You were the younger sister."

The younger sister! My mind raced to remember the Eliot family line.

"You were very talented."

Of course, it all made sense now! I *had* been a daughter in the Evans family. Mary Ann lost her mother while she was still living at home. Her father's voice was her moral voice after her mother died. She had no valid voice of her own until he passed away. Now that Dr. Cohen had nailed the theme of my circle of karma, it was easy to analyze this one for myself.

"Now, Freda, practice every day for the next thirty days to free your voice. Do the meditation in my book, and meet the child and free the child by loving and accepting the child unconditionally. You must work hard, especially on the life of the healer when you were burned at the stake. You were abandoned in all of these lives, and lost your voice in each. You must work to regain that voice in this life."

I sat silently wondering about what my daughter had said about my mother, her life, and her death.

"The Guides are again telling me that you have a question."

"Is my mother around me?" I shared the story of her early death.

"She is, and she is so present that she is almost palpable. She is crying."

"Why is she crying?"

"She didn't want to leave you, but she had to. She was also your mother in the French life—the mother who was an actress. She left her daughter twice, and she is so sorry for that. She wants you to know she was no angel—that she had faults too. She wants you to know that she loves you. Almost palpable!"

At that point I was weeping quietly, and wondering how to end the call well. The paper I had been using to make notes was spotted in tears.

"I'm going to close the call now, Freda, if there is nothing else."

"Of course...oh, yes, there is something else! There's a man I've been helping—with his book. Is there advice you might offer about getting it published?"

"His book? Why his book? Get *your* voice heard. This is most important for your life. He is a person from your past life as well. He is a good man now, as he was then. But you must concentrate on *you* now—your writing, your voice."

"Yes, you are right, Dr. Cohen. Thank you, and thank your Guides for me as well."

"Give yourself time—at least one time per day for thirty days to revisit the children who wait to be loved and accepted—those children who are you in past lives. Bless you, Freda, and goodbye."

"Goodbye, Dr. Cohen, and bless you too."

I was numb and unable to concentrate for some time. I prayed, I slept, I meditated, I read through Laski's *George Eliot* biography to try to figure out who the younger sister was in the Evans family line. It wasn't an immediate revelation. If I *had* been George Eliot in an earlier life, surely Dr. Cohen would have said so. Perhaps I was the young Mary Ann, and the George Eliot pseudonym caused confusion. Or maybe I'm the other sister, Chrissy. Can Guides get confused? Can a psychic reader make mistakes? They knew better than I.

To ground myself, I walked down the backstairs to the kitchen to wash the lunch dishes. This was an old habit of mine. If I felt anxious about something, I would put my hands to work. The lavender dishwashing suds were soothing. My mind continued to travel while my hands were scrubbing dishes and placing them in the opposite sink for rinsing. I was on auto pilot and had to do something to finalize the session. I went to my computer and translated the hand written notes from my session with Dr. Cohen. As I did, all I could think of were Dr. Heinemann's words forming in my head about taking what I need for this life and leaving the rest!

My attention drifted to another place in time. It was spring, and a fine mist of rain enveloped the manor. A friend of ours, Dr. Charles Ridley, had stayed the night. He was adamant about repaying the kindness by giving me a treatment. I led him to the Sanctuary Garden through the mist. It was the most peaceful place on our property, and if I was going to have a spiritual treatment, it was going to be there. Charles was a specialist in biodynamic cranial treatment. He had recently written a book titled *Stillness: Biodynamic Cranial Practice and the Evolution of Consciousness*. He taught the process around the world. His method was meditative with the intention of assisting with evolving consciousness. In addition, he had been a Buddhist monk for many years and was highly sensitive to energies.

The treatment was so natural that I hardly knew Charles was present. Almost immediately I saw bright white light at the top of my head. I lost the sensation of my body and rested inside my head where light seemed to be moving in and out of my crown area. When the session was over, Charles shared with me what he'd seen and experienced during the treatment.

"As I placed my hand on you, a deep stillness came over me that filled my inner body space with peace. Light breathed into and out of my body, ebbing and flowing like an ocean tide. When each infusion of light entered, it deepened the awareness of my inner body expanding into spaciousness toward the horizon. A feeling of sacred love permeated my inner body space, now vast and full of light, and I sensed a presence as though a blessing were taking place between you and the angels. It was then that I was struck with an inner knowing that you possessed the qualities of a saint."

Following the session with Dr. Ridley, I realized that my soul had already evolved to an extent. This knowledge helped me over a number of emotional humps. I rested in gratitude. We cannot be perfect. God knows I was not, and neither was George Eliot. We can continue to search, but we can also stop struggling and accept those things we do not understand. We live in a world of mystery, and yet our daily lives are caught-up with human priorities of survival. We are, for the most part, realists, and only a small percentage of us take the time to tune-in to the great mystery of life itself.

The mysteries presented to George Eliot were unlocked one by one until she held the key to her own life firmly in her hand. As young Mary Ann Evans, she learned about phrenology from the Bray's friend, Dr. George Combe. Much was learned from her evaluation and head cast. It revealed why she was said to have the intellect of a man. According to Charles Bray, Eliot had the skull features of Dante. In fact, one profile drawing of her in Marghanita Laski's *George Eliot* biography looks very much like Dante. She kept a painting of the author among her house possessions. Eliot had always admired Dante's writings. In addition, she may have felt akin to him as a result of her phrenology reading.

I wondered what would surface next to align me with Eliot. How could this knowledge help me—the world around me? Would the revelations confirm that there is nothing new, and that lives, circumstances, and even personalities repeat themselves through time? Or do we each have an archetype as Caroline Myss believes? *Is George Eliot living in a parallel universe while I am here as a kind of twin born a dimension away?*

Freda M. Chaney

–9–

Evans Genealogy

B ed and Breakfast guests had come and gone during the summer. They noticed a "different" host. One lovely lady who'd made repeated visits said that she suspicioned there were two sides of Freda, and wanted to know the "secret" I was hiding. Was it that obvious? Another guest said she thought I was a "channel" bringing spiritual healing for those who visited the manor. A couple who came for their honeymoon said things felt "magical" at the manor. The new husband and wife had been out on the lawn taking photos, and orbs appeared in their pictures. I tried taking photos of them with my own camera, but the orbs only multiplied.

I was compelled to take more and more orb photos. I had to see what was in them—if there was a message in them as Dr. Heinemann believed. My picture files were littered with orbs—morning, noon, and nighttime orbs; colored orbs, bright white orbs, orbs with concentric circles, some with sections missing like a slice out of a pie. There were orbs that appeared to have human faces, orbs that looked as though a group of people was peering down through a large telescope. There were orbs with pets, and finally orbs that acted as though they were conscious of their actions, appearing on flowers as though sniffing the scent of a lily, and one was checking out Sadie's backside! I went through two cameras within months. I thought perhaps my older camera was producing anomalies, so I purchased a more sophisticated one. There were still orbs!

I needed a vacation from myself! Or from Eliot! Or both! I was zoned between some moment of reality in my own life at the manor, and some other reality involving George Eliot's family. The past life reading clarified that I was born into her family in the past. I had to learn who the younger sister was, or go mad!

What I discovered during another look into George Eliot's biography was that Mary Ann Evans, in fact, *was* the younger sister! She was the youngest of five living children born to two different mothers and the same father. Robert Evans, Mary Ann's father, married again when his first wife died. There were two children by the first marriage: Robert (b.1802) and Lucy, also known as Fanny (b.1805). To the second marriage were born three children, a boy and two girls: Chrissy (b. 1814), Isaac (b.1816), and Mary Ann (b. 1819). The younger sister of that second marriage *was* Mary Ann—George Eliot! Mary Ann's older sister was Chrissy.

Twin boys were born between Chrissy's birth and Mary Ann's, but they did not survive. Robert Evans Jr., Mr. Evans first born son, had already started a life of his own by the time his father started his second family. Fanny, the eldest daughter, moved in with her brother, Robert, so that Mr. Evans and his new wife, Christiana, could start a new family of their own. Suddenly, it dawned on me that I was also a sibling from a family of five, born of two different mothers. The more I thought about it, the more I was sure that I was being shown these parallels for a reason. The path through Eliot's life was also the path through the mystery of my own life.

Suddenly, I wanted to know more about my own genealogy. I remembered a cousin had sent me dozens of photos. I switched on my computer and looked through photo files. For an hour I sat staring at the screen watching thumbnail photos flip by. Then I saw one with the caption "Great Grandfather Evans." I hadn't remembered there were Evans in our family. I clicked the photo file and onto the viewing screen appeared a sepia tone photo of my maternal Great Grandfather, Joseph Evans. How coincidental could it be that Eliot's surname and my ancestor's was the same? Joseph Evans looked quite handsome in a suit and tie. It appeared the photo had been taken when he was young. I began to imagine what he must have been like—if he was a good husband and father—strong, but kind.

I pored over photos until my eyes were begging for rest. Just before switching off the computer, I saw a photo of a woman with her white hair swept up in a knot. She was wearing a print dress with a brooch pinned into the bodice. Her face was deeply wrinkled. No makeup accentuated her obviously Native American features. Her eyes were deep set, but soft. I knew this person to be the woman our family called Ma, Great Grandmother Odecy. Joseph Evans had married Odecy in Kentucky. He preceded her in death. Ma lived to be ninety-three years old, outliving a few husbands. *Could my Evans family genealogy somehow be connected to Mary Ann Evans' family?*

So many questions! Not only had I felt like an orphan all of my life, but here I was searching in my mother's background that was a mystery to me. I knew little about my Great Grandmother Odecy Evans, and nothing about her husband, Joseph. There had been a disconnection between families following my mother's death. When my father remarried, he left the home he'd built for my mother, and moved us all to a sixty acre farm, leaving behind the modest block structure, the treacherous hillside on which it stood, and the overseeing eye of my mother's family. Never did my grandparents imagine their daughter would die at twenty-six, and even more horrifying was the reality of also losing touch with her children. The last time I saw my grandfather he was leaning over a fence calling out my name, and I was forbidden by my parents to go to him. The distance, the time, the death of Grandfather Henry—all culminated in a lifelong pain that knitted itself deeply inside my soul.

In primary school, we read a story titled *The Little Match Girl* by Hans Christian Andersen. I wept quietly as we read. It described my yearning for family so accurately that it sent an arrow straight to my heart. And now to unfold the mystery of how Eliot was associated with me, I had to open the wound which had somehow healed after several failed relationships and miserable attempts at becoming a whole being. But the little match girl who died outside of the warm and happy house had been holding her last flaming match to offer light to a dark world. It was my turn to do the same, and George Eliot would play an integral part in shedding light onto a sad and sometimes sickened world that tends to forget its own.

Mary Ann had struggled as a child, trying to prove herself more than just another little girl who needed to follow rigid rules of gentility. She was born into a culture suited for the servitude of men and God, and though she tried to serve both, devoting great emotional willpower, she failed. She failed because she was a woman who could shine—beyond herself, her family ties, her time period. She could shine her light in spite of her physical ugliness. She could shine her light in spite of the fact that she was "different" in the eyes of her school peers. I would see to it that her light would shine even more brilliantly through me because I understood how Eliot felt. Inside, I am that little girl full of longing, lighting my last match to keep warm my hopes for understanding, acceptance, and empathy.

I was determined to find what I was searching for in some small antique shop littered with gaudy Victorian postcards, in the yellowed letters tucked into wax sealed envelopes, in the eyes of passers-by in Nuneaton, Eliot's birthplace. Out there—out beyond the confines of mere human reasoning was the payload. Out there, I would find myself!

Facing the south window, I saw mourning doves resting on the split seam metal roof. Two sitting side-by-side: George and George? Lewes and Eliot? I smiled to myself. I had always loved doves. I once took one in when I found it had a broken wing. For six months, I nursed it back to health, and in the spring, I opened the basement window and watched it fly. I wrote a poem about the experience titled *Dove with Broken Wing*. The female dove had lived in the smothering gray of the basement all winter, alighting on the small ground level window seeking escape. It reminds me of a song titled "Radiant Dark," from the long poem, *The Spanish Gypsy* by George Eliot:

Dark the night, with breath all flow'rs,

And tender broken voice that fills

With ravishment the listening hours:

Whisperings, wooings,

Liquid ripples and soft ring-dove cooings

In low-toned rhythm that love's aching stills.

Everything was coming up Eliot! Perhaps I was off on a metaphor mind trip, following a riveted path and placing focus on every detail as Eliot herself had done! Her mind, of necessity, was trained for details. When traveling, she would focus her attention, first with her eyes and then with her heart: the cultural richness, its intrinsic charm, its rustic, rugged, and pitiful aspects, committing to memory the fragments that would become classics in British literature. Perhaps this was my gift from the gods as well—this intense perception of the world around me. Like Eliot, I had made the most of my gift through writing. She had mastered realism in novels. Thus far, I had shared my gift through non-fiction and poetry.

It was difficult staying grounded knowing I was walking a path right into the nineteenth century, but my husband knew just when to step into my office and remind me of who I was, and what my duties were. Somehow, like Eliot's soulmate, he had the intuition for seeing ahead. His to-do lists were posted in every area of the house, but particularly on his huge oak desk. Everything was compartmentalized—had its place. Pigeon-holed! I was the butterfly with an ethereal sense that I was something more than what the solidity of the physical plane offered. Norm represented perfectly the grounding that Lewes brought for George Eliot.

I enjoyed being home. The manor grounds were like Eden to me. I was perfectly at peace surrounded by nature. Norm was the one who liked shopping and running errands. My father had a vulgar term for going off in the car too often. He'd accuse my stepmother of it. When I did join Norm on an outing, I would read to him as he drove—something we both loved. On our honeymoon, I read *Riders of the Purple Sage* by Zane Grey. I can't say we loved that one, but we laughed until our sides hurt! Some thought it was not good for me to stay at home so much, but I had plenty to keep me busy, especially now. I had research to do and a shocking book to write!

I continued researching my Evans family genealogy. My Great Grandfather, Joseph Evans, was born in 1860, the same year that Eliot published *The Mill on the Floss*. Among the dog-eared pages accented with pencil, ink, and bright yellow highlighter, there was a stapled collection of papers dated August 10, 2005. The date struck me as the day my mother had passed away fifty-one years before. The inside address was from my cousin who was the devoted genealogist in our family. She had interviewed her father about my mother, Lois, and our great grandmother, Odecy. The collected pages were the result of that interview. I lifted the papers and read:

> Lois didn't have electricity until she married. When she was growing up, they used wood cook stoves and kerosene lanterns for lights. Iceboxes held fifty pound blocks of ice. She used Toni home permanents to curl her hair. She heated evaporated milk cans on the stove and knocked the ends out with a knife. Then she cut the cans into quarter inch strips and wrapped them in newspaper, rolled her hair in them, and then folded the ends of the strips over her hair.

Though the interview notes were sparse and had no literary merit, I learned, as though from a Bible, what a hard life my mother had lived, and how she loved in spite of it. I wondered how much more I could read before breaking into tears for her. It seemed I was living the life she deserved to live—with automatic everything: hair curlers and straighteners, dishwashers, electric washers and dryers. My mother, a woman trapped by her illness had never had a driver's license. How dependent she must have felt on others around her. As I continued to read, tears fell. I was reading about my mother—a real person just like me.

"Your mom's notebook of songs was a two ring binder with lined paper inside. She listened to the radio and wrote down the songs she liked."

In her own way, my mother was a writer. My uncle noted that she had been good at her school work. What little evidence there was of her ability to write was a baby book meticulously kept for my older brothers. I always wondered why my mother had not started a baby book for me. Perhaps she was just too ill, and too busy with three children to devote herself to the task. It was a sad fact that there were no photos of us together, and no photographic evidence of her having taken joy in the moment of my arrival. All that existed was a birth certificate with my inked footprints and her thumbprints. My whole world existed on that one piece of paper, and something my father told me about the night she was in the hospital delivering me. He said that even while she was in labor she was laughing out loud with other ladies in the birthing ward. It made me feel good to know she was looking forward to my birth, and that my delivery had not caused her too much agony.

I read on to learn about the world of Great Grandmother Odecy Evans. Curiously, her husband, Joseph Evans must have died fairly young, since he was not mentioned in the interview. Odecy had lived in the hills of Kentucky, raising her family as best she could. There were fond tales of her woven through the family tapestry. It seems she had a sweet tooth and was always making fudge with copious amounts of local black walnuts. Rumor had it that Odecy hid peppermint candy in her suitcase when she went for distant family visits. When little ones of the host's household discovered the candy, she refused to share with them.

The interview also noted that Odecy prepared sauerkraut in huge crocks, cutting the cabbage into large chunks, adding vinegar and spices, and allowing it to ferment in the basement. Odecy's green grape pie was another curious gastronomical experiment she pulled off beautifully. One day when berries couldn't be found for her favorite cobblers, she whipped up a green grape pie appreciated by all who were fortunate enough to get a slice. I tried to imagine how sour a green grape pie might taste, and how slimy the grapes would feel inside a pie crust. I could appreciate Great Grandma Odecy's make-do mountain spirit. She was an innovator.

Hominy was her specialty. She would leach the livestock feed-corn with lye to remove the hard outer shell and puff the kernel. Then she'd boil the kernels in water for twelve to eighteen hours to remove the lye. She had hillbilly know-how for wintering-over apples and pears in her basement, for storing sundry root vegetables, and was most likely a local master at hunting herbs and medicinal roots in the hills of Kentucky. It occurred to me that Mary Ann might have learned some of the same preserving and cooking methods as those of my great grandmother.

In addition to kitchen skills, my Grandmother Odecy Evans was a midwife to many. She had birthed most of her grandchildren. The one she did not midwife was lost at the hands of a local doctor. The time period was full of self-reliance, though not quite pioneer life. The exquisite studio photo of Great Grandmother Odecy made it obvious to me that even though her circumstances were primitive, she did her best to be ladylike in less than genteel surroundings with her upswept hair, the beautiful print dress, and Victorian brooch.

There was nothing in the interview between my uncle and cousin that would indicate we had Evans relations in England. I had to move on and learn more about Eliot. I felt I knew her as this young lady who had lived a typical country lifestyle. I could almost smell her mince pies as they cooled on the pantry shelf near the Griff House kitchen. To think of her there made me feel at home in the same way baking made me feel in my own manor house kitchen. By modern standards, even I was living primitively in my drafty old house. Perhaps even that would be considered odd by modern women who lived without a pantry or basement, whose houses were perched on concrete slabs and decorated in a "less is more" style. Should I invite them to tea—a literary tea where we might all sit in book club fashion to discuss our readings of George Eliot? I could serve cucumber sandwiches, shortbread triangles, mince tarts, and strong tea. As we crunched and munched through the meeting, we would discover George Eliot through her plots, characters, and settings one delicious book at a time. Onward then!

Part 2

∞ Literary Leanings ∞

–10–

The Mill Stone

What a great day for literary lunacy! Once again I was tripping through metaphors and mind games. Returning to the exquisitely detailed Heritage Club edition of *The Mill on the Floss*, I gently lifted each page to read the whimsical words of George Eliot. Each time I held it, it seemed heavier as though the weight of two lives, two authors, two tormented thinkers were sharing experiences within its pages. It was her book, but it was my life I was reading about. It was my heart breaking when Tom shouted that he hated Maggie for allowing his rabbits to die. I felt the tears that dropped to Maggie's starched white pinafore. It was my hair matted in mud from playing along the Floss River bank. The déjà vu sharing of experiences never ended from one chapter to the next.

Here I was with this knowledge of someone else's life like a mill stone around my neck, but only able to share it with a few. Even in that respect I was like George Eliot and her autobiographical character, Maggie, having to hide thoughts, feelings, and my excitement to share what I learned. I set the thick clothbound book aside, and walked to my office bookshelves. I could sometimes sense the right book for just the right moment. I pulled down *The Tenth Insight: Holding the Vision* by James Redfield. I pushed my reading glasses tighter onto the bridge of my nose. Redfield said,

> As our trust of the spiritual increases, we step back and comprehend our experiences of intuition and coincidence. When seemingly incredible coincidences occur to lead us forward, we perceive that these poignant moments are somehow predestined.

I wondered where I could go with my "coincidental" experiences. I could lie in the attic as Maggie did, but I had always lived life radically—full speed ahead with hair flying. Oh, but that was just the young Maggie who sobbed and sulked in the attic, her chin lost under a protruding lower lip. She—and I had matured.

Reluctantly, I placed Redfield's timely book back on the shelf and returned to reading *The Mill on the Floss* with new purpose. My trust in the spiritual *had* increased. I was experiencing synchronicity daily, and now I was stepping back to comprehend what those spiritual experiences had brought to my life. I had learned through Dr. Cohen that my mission for this life was to make my voice heard. I tried to stay in touch with friends and family, but perhaps George Eliot had more in mind for me. The balance of my destiny might lie in the pages of her books, especially her early novel, *The Mill on the Floss*.

I sat on my Victorian bed, propped by a bolster pillow, again holding the book that had turned my whole world upside down. I suddenly felt like Victoria Holt in the movie *Déjà vu* when she realized something happened in Paris that made her feel out of sync with her learned reality. The beautiful blonde woman, the bistro, the jeweled pin— everything seemed physical, and yet it was outside of the physical reality she'd known just moments before.

I think I had pushed the button for the twelfth floor only to find that the elevator went directly to floor thirteen! What does one do when the elevator stops at the thirteenth floor? Do they grip the rail and stand weak-kneed at the back of the elevator, or step off to see where it goes? I had the plot of someone else's life to learn now, just when I thought I had my own life plot almost figured out.

The character, Maggie, was the odd rebellious exception to the otherwise solidified, patriarchy of the Tulliver family. She was a precocious child who emulated her brother in all he did. Resenting all attempts to make her into a lady like her cousin Lucy, Maggie defied her aunts, her mother, her brother, and society in general. Here we see an autobiographical snapshot of young Mary Ann Evans. Maggie was sent off to a boarding school for girls, while Tom, her older brother, was given a premium education for which he was neither qualified nor appreciative. Maggie grew by leaps and bounds through all of the adversities that life could muster, while Tom fell into the typical Tulliver family rut of judgment, resentment, and lack of forgiveness. Young Mary Ann and I both seemed to be on the deficit side when it came to familial consideration, but nonetheless at the top of our game at getting on in life.

I had been a precocious child too, always investigating, educating myself in lofty pursuits. I was writing at the age twelve, planning a writing career at sixteen, and publishing my first poetry at twenty two. One would think I got there by family support, but at every step there were fretful fingers attempting to pull me back from my meeting with destiny. I was a carbon copy of the character, Maggie, in that respect. So many of the clannish rules that hindered Maggie in her childhood also hindered me.

Continuing to unravel the plot of *The Mill on the Floss*, I learned that Maggie's father, Edward Tulliver, was known as an honest, hardworking man who could also be proud, stubborn, and quarrelsome. The latter character attributes do not describe Eliot's own father who was even-tempered and respected in Warwickshire. The character Maggie adored her father. Eliot loved and respected her father as well. I also knew my father was special when I was very young. No matter his rough edges, he kept us all together after our mother died.

Maggie lost her father when she was young. It was devastating to her because of their close relationship. Mary Ann lost her mother when she was fifteen. In the novel, she simply reversed the roles. Eliot and I were both severely affected by the early loss of a parent.

In *The Mill on the Floss*, the autobiographical brother, Tom, tolerated Maggie, while showing fondness for her in his own way. Maggie emulated Tom and was deeply affected by his rejection of her. One of my brothers was a playmate for me since we were close in age. I was a dyed-in-the-wool tomboy, climbing trees, learning simple auto mechanics, and drag racing along a straight stretch near our home. If the character, Maggie, lived in modern times, she no doubt would have been in blue jeans and pigtails, twisting a wrench under the hood of Tom's car. My brother could be sweet, but his periodic disappearing act was an umbrella over any possibilities for a positive relationship. It was the way of things in our family—the mark of clan mentality—who's in, who's out. For the most part, I was "out" because I was so different from the rest of the clan.

Maggie loved Philip Wakem, a hunchback who was bright, talented, and friendly. Philip's father was a social enemy of the Tulliver family, and thus a Romeo and Juliet theme emerged. Philip's father threatened to block the use of the Floss River tributary that fed into the mill where the Tullivers made their living. While Mr. Tulliver and Mr. Wakem drew their battle lines and young Tom joined in, Maggie and Philip found companionship together. This mutual admiration did not fully evolve because the "Tybalt" of the Tulliver family, Tom, fought to defend his sister, Maggie. Tom's anxiety did not extend from the actual relationship of the two, but from old family-feud positions, that he was bound to uphold, having sworn a sacred oath to his dying father. Tom condemned Maggie for her relationship with Philip, even though Tom had also been a friend of the hunchback. Maggie decided to stop seeing Philip to spare her relationship with her brother. Her sacrifice was in vain, and her reunification with Tom short-lived.

Maggie was completely rejected and thrown out of the family home by Tom when Lucy's fiancé, Stephen, kept her out overnight bringing shame on the Tulliver family. No manner of pleading would convince Tom to forgive Maggie. Unmarried, with no prospects of which Tom would approve, Maggie survived the circumstances by taking a room, and looking for employment so that she would not be dependent on her mother. Clergyman Kenn offered her the position as governess. Things seemed to be looking up for Maggie, but in no time gossip began circulating about a supposed attraction between Maggie and Clergyman Kenn. She left her employment at his request. She was devastated, but understood that Clergyman Kenn wanted to prevent more malicious gossip. She had lost her last, best hope of being independent.

In the final scene of *The Mill on the Floss,* Maggie rowed to Dorlcote Mill when she saw that the flood waters were rising. Her intent was to rescue her brother, forgive his unkindness toward her, and find her way back into his heart. Maggie took on the St. Teresa role of sacrifice for others, giving all, and receiving little or nothing in return. I was shocked to read that Maggie and her brother died together in the boat while they rowed against the wild current full of debris.

It was too much to digest immediately. Memories were pressing me. I was sifting and sorting through a lifetime of thoughts, pain, and pleasures trying to make sense of it all. Like Maggie, I too had been friends with a gentleman who had a spinal deformity. My story of sacrifice, love, and loss was remarkably similar to that of Eliot's autobiographical character, Maggie. I was the forgiving sister, the penitent daughter, the diminished woman who never quite found her place in a male-dominated society. The water parallels were powerful too. Maggie died in the Floss River immediately after forgiving Tom, ending the painful silence between them. Eliot died in her new home along the Thames River at #4 Cheyne Walk, having just ended her years-long estrangement from her brother, Isaac. It would seem that Eliot had masterfully written the final scene for her own life!

I had my own near-drowning experience when I was a teenager. I was out rowing with three friends in a small lake which was overshadowed by a huge oak tree. Suddenly, a young boy shouted from the shore that the tree was falling. We looked up to see the oak as stable as ever. We assumed the boy was joking. *Who was he? Where did he come from?* Suddenly the oak tree came crashing into the lake, pinning the back of our boat. *How did the boy know the tree was about to fall?* The water, which had been serene just moments before, was now full of choppy waves. Our boat was pinned by branches and taking on water. I wrestled the branches off the back of the boat, and somehow we managed to row the boat to shore. We never saw the little boy again. *Guideposts Angels on Earth* magazine published my story in 1996.

I felt confused—like I had entered a multi-dimensional doorway where the arrow *was indeed* pointing to floor thirteen, and I would have to make a decision to get off and investigate the landscape of "seem," or grip the rail of physical reality and continue to sweat bullets. Anyone might feel this way given the circumstances. Who was I? Was I myself? Was I the character Maggie? Was I Eliot in control of all of these elements? I was beginning to think we were all characters in a master plot being woven through lifetimes like Eliot's master work of *Middlemarch*—weaving lives, and hopes, and dreams into an intricate and complicated web of human dialectic.

-11-

Middlemarching

M y view of reality had been challenged during the reading of *The Mill on the Floss*. It was too close to home. Now for some *Middlemarch* madness! Since this novel was Eliot's most popular, I read it next. I had a copy on the shelf, a 2003 Barnes and Noble Classics version with a handy and thorough timeline, "The World of George Eliot and Middlemarch," and an informative Introduction by Lynne Sharon Schwartz.

Already, I was enjoying this book more than *The Mill on the Floss*. The tome was as heavy as a cheese wagon making rounds through the Midlands of England. It was rich, and the characters came in all shapes and sizes, some with voluminous holes (faults) that somehow complemented them like a fine Swiss cheese, yet they worked together like they'd been glued with mucilage. It was as though Eliot had crammed every character she had ever met or imagined between book covers and dared them to dance without music! The sins of the so-called "righteous" served to highlight the philosophical integrity of Dorothea. She held a candle for me, bidding me to follow her home to the real George Eliot—the heart that perhaps only her soulmate, George Lewes, really knew.

Middlemarch was based on two main characters rather than a single protagonist. Dorothea was a saint, working quietly, yet heroically behind the scenes for her husband, the scholarly Edward Casaubon. She relished the role of doing some good through supporting her husband in his vain attempts to create his masterpiece, "The Key to All Mythologies." Being an idealist at heart, Dorothea became weary of the narrow class views of her husband and his harsh judgment upon his young cousin, Will Ladislaw, a Byronic, hot-tempered, artistic type whom Dorothea grew to love, revealing her feelings in the final scenes of the novel.

There was another *Middlemarch* protagonist with a lofty, hybrid name, Tertius Lydgate, a young doctor who was also an idealist. He worked long hours without pay to relieve patients' suffering. Dr. Lydgate was proud and priggish in a male-dominated society, risking his marriage to Rosamond to proclaim his authority as head of household over his wife. The two protagonists, Dorothea Casaubon and Dr. Lydgate, though quite different from one another, especially in their levels of humility, were much alike in speaking their opinions about the social inequities of life in the 1830s. They balanced one another in word and deed. Lydgate needed saving, and Dorothea desperately needed someone to save. I wondered what might have happened had George Eliot brought Tertius and Dorothea together to be wed instead of to their equally unsuitable mates. But then there wouldn't be the show-stopping love scene at the end of the novel when at long last Will and Dorothea kiss. Heaven forbid!

I pondered the two characters, comparing my own idealist thinking—the troubles I'd gotten myself into when speaking up too soon, or writing the editorial that got the town talking. I had always been one to stand up for the disenfranchised. Eliot had the same penchant for speaking out, saying the truth, revealing injustice in the society she knew. Again, I was feeling the weaving of lives and events and characters in *Middlemarch* that had confronted me in *The Mill on the Floss*. *Middlemarch*, however, was a grand literary lacing of provincial lives where her earlier novel had been a simple community patchwork quilt. *Middlemarch* was deliciously sophisticated and active in its constant movement surrounding characters' lives, and political and historical events of the period.

I read an archived *Middlemarch* book review by Henry James (www.complete-review.com), originally published in the *Galaxy* in March 1873. He criticized *Middlemarch*, suggesting that it seemed contrived. He appreciated her earlier work for its simplicity and raw emotion. It was well known that Eliot traveled and studied other cultures and locales with a keen eye. She was also an avid reader, and the rich details in *Middlemarch* would have reflected that vast knowledge. *Middlemarch* is rich, complicated, and expansive in scope because of its dual protagonists which began as single heroes for two separate books that Eliot later combined.

In addition, the landscapes differed greatly from one of Eliot's novels to the next. *Middlemarch* was a bustling town on the verge of railroads and industry. The classes ranged from lower to middle to aristocratic. A rich interaction of characters would take place under such circumstances. *Middlemarch* provided a bustling modern setting for ambitious new political leaders looking to fill seats in Parliament. The big issue at that time was the Reform Bill of 1832, which intended to give the middle class the right to vote. To compare *Middlemarch* to a modern novel, I think it might measure up to the sweeping sagas, *Gone with the Wind* by Margaret Mitchell, or *The Thorn Birds* by Colleen McCullough. If Henry James were living in modern times, even he might have a different opinion of *Middlemarch* with its popularity as strong now as it was when it was first released. So there you have it, Mr. James!

I laid the novel aside, and stretched. It was nearly 6:00 p.m. My head was swimming with details. I slipped on my gardening boots, called Sadie, and stepped out for fresh air. A breeze was blowing the dark scent of aromatic herbs up around the manor house. I stooped to get a closer glimpse at the sweet woodruff. Only such a vigorous, substantial herb as this could choke out mint! There were a few surviving mint plants trailing around the pots and flagstone steps. My kitchen garden greeted guests each year with an earthy, overgrown welcome. Reaching down, I pulled a leaf and rubbed it between my thumb and forefinger. Its pungency was inviting after "sitting so long in one attitude" as Jane Austen would say. I spotted some lemon balm and picked that too. Bringing it up to my nose, I reveled in the brightness of its scent.

I planted rose geranium herb once, and marveled at its ability to capture me at the house corner—its strong, ambitious scent wafting out like hands to lure me in. I dried the huge stalks in the basement that fall, and though the plant lost its supple velvet appearance, it did not lose its pungency. What a treat it was to go searching in the cool basement for canned goods knowing the scent of dried rose geranium would greet me at the bottom of the stairs. Surely Eliot had dried and stored herbs at the Griff House. Herbs certainly would have figured into their country fare of stews, lamb roasts, hearty potato dishes, and seasoned breads. Eliot was known to take long walks in the country, noting the wildflowers along the way.

Holding my cluster of herbs in a tussie mussie fashion, I whistled for Sadie to follow. I made my way into the Sanctuary Garden and up into the pasture fields made quaint with hanging gates and leaning fence posts. A bluebird box was inhabited, and so was the purple martin house that Norm had built. However, the tenants were not martins, but sparrows. Norm would be disappointed again this year. I rounded the barn on the north side and walked over the little foot bridge to the kidney-shaped pond. Sadie was reluctant to follow me onto the dock, and surveyed the nearby orchard instead. Looking out over the water, I spotted one of the white amur fish coming to the surface with a decided splash. A dragonfly winged by my head, and in the distance a great blue heron flew in a path to its favorite south pond belonging to our neighbors. It was more secluded there, and had no pollutants from the neighbor's chemical yard treatments. That didn't seem to bother the fish, frogs, and small aquatic birds on our property, but the herons weren't so fond.

Peering at my reflection in the pond, I almost expected to see the face of Eliot staring back at me. But all I saw were bobbing clouds and a wavy view of myself in a light blue kitchen dress. Somehow I looked like someone who was looking at water for the first time—like the cave men must have looked when they first discovered fire. I had been in the house too long, head buried in books, and split down the middle of myself and Eliot. I sat at the edge of the dock and hung my feet, still in gardening wellies, over the edge, swinging them in rhythmic motion like pumping a childhood swing. My mind drifted off to other times, other places.

The moon hung in a wide arc in the early evening sky. It was oddly obvious at that hour. In the western field, a whippoorwill sounded, and a small herd of white-tailed deer moved cautiously along a tree line, nibbling around cornstalks as they went. I stared at the streambed, the leaning corn crib, the intrusive flashing cell tower light on the right side of the road. What would Eliot have said about the intrusive "progress" of modern man?

It seemed clear from my readings, that Eliot loved nature, especially water. Water was the predominant natural element in *The Mill on the Floss*. I reviewed the book plot in my mind. The mill was everything to the Tullivers—their livelihood and source of pride. When the mill was lost, bitter tears were wept and combined with promises of revenge. Maggie Tulliver and Phillip Wakem secretly met near the water's edge sharing lovely afternoons unbeknownst to Maggie's family. When Stephen Guest lured Maggie to the boat and tried to seduce her, Maggie was both passionate and outraged, and the water on which the boat had floated serenely suddenly became a broken dam of emotions. Later, when Maggie rowed toward the mill to save her brother, Tom, she fought the very water that had been so meaningful to her in childhood, integral to her fondest memories. She managed to stay afloat until her brother was onboard, and just as Tom made amends to Maggie, the boat capsized from floating debris. The two were taken down into the deep water.

Where *The Mill on the Floss* depended on the old ways of making a living and family traditions, *Middlemarch* introduced progress both as something to be embraced and something to be resisted. Nature is the first to succumb to progress, but without progress there is natural entropy that brings a town to its knees. Eliot seemed to be for progress, but in a slow, deliberate way. Her *Middlemarch* protagonist, Dorothea, was quite at home in the country and without the trappings of extravagance that progress seemed to offer. One might look through a modern window and view similar reflections of the same thoughts of progress between the separated panes of time.

-12-

The Simplicity of Silas

Much to my delight, *Silas Marner* was direct and refreshing. I have a great appreciation for the humanitarian aspects of the little book. I could relate to the way Eliot made her readers consider the human condition in a thousand and one ways. She could take a character and turn her or him inside out—an angel one moment and a demon the next. Clearly Eliot believed in redemption—brought her characters to the threshold—and shoved them through the eye of a reader's humanity.

Certainly Eliot's readers teetered on the brink, seeing a condemned Silas Marner—the miser weaver who was given to trances, depression, and reclusiveness—suddenly redeemed fully from the sin he didn't commit! Truly, Marner was a type of Christ as was the child, Eppie. Marner is accused unjustly, and still he manages to go on with his work and life, accepting the help of his neighbors when Eppie wanders into his life. Eliot is teaching a moral lesson. When Silas' gold is stolen, he is vulnerable and confused. His fortune in gold—what had meant most to him—was gone.

Then Eppie, a motherless child who wanders to his doorstep, answers his deepest need for companionship, loyalty, and unconditional love. In turn, Eppie has the best kind of friend in Silas who gives her a simple, but sheltered life.

Eppie was born into a secret marriage between an aristocratic gentleman, Godfrey, and his lower class wife, Molly. She was spared only by the death of her drug-addicted mother, and the willingness of her father to allow Eppie to remain with Marner. Gold was given to seal the deal and to ease the wealthy father's conscience. Marner's fortune being restored, he could provide well for Eppie. The child represents purity arising from impure circumstances. Her father, who married a second time into his own aristocratic class, remained childless, perhaps reparation for sins against his first wife.

I could identify my own life in this story—with the simplicity of my childhood lifestyle, the loss of my mother, and my father as a single parent of the household for a time. Eliot could also relate to these circumstances, and had most likely created an autobiographical sketch of her life through the characters.

By the time Eliot wrote *Silas Marner*, she was already famous. She had been stunned by her sudden rise to fame following a lifetime of rejection. *Silas Marner* wasn't to be the most loved novel, but it may have been a novel that drove her to look at her life through a magnifying glass: the money she'd earned, the "husband" she was sharing with Agnes Lewes who had never been legally divorced from George Lewes, her decision not to have children of her own, and her great attachment to Lewes' children as some kind of recompense—all collectively foreshadowing the characters and their evolution through the book.

Following the popularity of *Adam Bede* and *The Mill on the Floss,* Eliot continued to have serious doubts about her ability to please her readers with her future work. As well, she questioned whether she deserved the good things in her life, and wondered if she might lose them as she'd lost so much in her life. Most of the men in Eliot's life treated her little better than Eppie's mother had been treated. What would become of her, and could she trust and accept Lewes' children—would they trust her? Could they be part of her redemption?

In the Introduction of the *Silas Marner* Signet Classic edition, 1999, Fredrick Karl remarks that much of the activity in the story revolves around the weaver's hearth. The classical role of the hearth is a holy place where gods are honored because they provided protection for the residents. Marghanita Laski wrote in her *George Eliot* biography that Eliot was drawn to the warmth of the fender at the fireplace. When we first moved to our home, we noticed that one of the statues was holding a flaming torch. Norm said this statue might be Hestia, goddess of the hearth. Over the years, our little fireplace had kept our kitchen cozy, and served as our sole source of heat when the electric power failed. At those times, we even cooked over the flames as Silas Marner had.

Eliot brought the characters 'round right at the end, and offered a satisfying conclusion to the heartache the novel initiated. Eppie stayed with Marner even though she learned she was the daughter of a wealthy aristocrat. In this, Marner and Eppie are both blessed. She ends the curse of generations by refusing to repeat her mother's mistake. She has chosen good karma by making wise choices. She will not mix with aristocracy lest she lose what is most important to her—the small comforts and the ordinary hero she has in Silas.

I felt consoled by this tiny gem of a book. In a brief space, Eliot shared that if we do our best and never give up, no matter what others are saying about us, in the end it will work out. Eliot's own experiences in life had proven this to be true. No matter how many men turned her away because she lacked physical beauty, she never stopped trying to find companionship. Though the world judged her severely for her eventual choice in Lewes, the relationship was right for her and for him. They had found in each other an intellectual and spiritual match. She was able to survive and thrive in his presence, and suddenly what the world laid as judgment at her feet, became the stepping stones to her fame as an author of fiction. And in Marner, she shares the perfect example of a man judged by society, cast away, and finally redeemed by another person—in his case, Eppie.

My own life had not been without issues of scorn. From the beginning, I could not live up to my mother's image. Since she died shortly after I was born, I bore the brunt of her death. And because I was the only daughter, I was expected to follow in her footsteps. Without my mother, that was difficult. There was a hollow spot deep in my soul that could not be filled. I attempted to banish the pain through relationships, but it didn't work—not until I found Norm. When Norm said to me that he knew my worth, I felt the pain of a lifetime beginning to subside. Like Eliot with Lewes, my relationship with Norm was treated with ridicule by some. The old saying that "the proof is in the pudding" applied to Eliot's life and my own. Both Eliot and I had met our soulmates, and neither of us minded the ridicule and judgment as long as we were together—finding purpose in a shared life.

Freda M. Chaney

-13-

Veiled!

Eliot could sometimes be slippery! You could define her one moment, and the next, she would morph beyond your radar. Imagine my surprise as I read Eliot's novella incorporating metaphysical elements. Eliot achieved almost everything she set her hand to, and this metaphysical short novel was just one more thing that Eliot threw at the shocked world in which she lived.

I pulled a footstool closer to the high back chair at the kitchen hearth. The flames cast eerie shadows on the bricks. Eliot could never get warm enough, and neither could I. She would love our manor house with fireplaces in almost every room, and our old fashioned hot water bottle at the ready to soothe cold feet.

Lifting a cup of British blend tea, I savored the aroma. It was stout enough to hold up to cream. The 1999 Oxford Classic paperback edition of Eliot's *The Lifted Veil* was stowed in my sweater pocket. It was a wonderful evening. Norm was sleeping in his favorite brown tweed chair, Sadie lay snoring contentedly near my feet, and Eliot waited to entertain me from my fireside seat.

In the Introduction of *The Lifted Veil*, Helen Small offers much information about Eliot and her novella. Many saw it as an odd book compared to Eliot's heretofore straightforward *Adam Bede* written in 1859. In fact, John Blackwood and Sons, Eliot's publisher, declined to represent the work at first. George Eliot used the term "double-consciousness," in reference to Latimer's mental condition, though it seemed to me that Latimer had extra sensory perception rather than mental illness. Small pointed out that Eliot used the same pliable, unscientific term, "double-consciousness," to describe herself in her 1860 travel journal. Eliot said,

> One great deduction to me from the delight of seeing world famous objects is the frequent double-consciousness which tells me that I am not enjoying the actual vision enough, and that when higher enjoyment comes with the reproduction of the scene in my imagination, I shall have lost some of the details, which impress me too feebly in the present because the faculties are not wrought up into energetic action.

In addition, Herbert Spencer, George Eliot's (then Marian Evans) eccentric, philosophical friend with whom she partnered to attend operas and theatre in 1852, wrote in his book, *An Autobiography,* that he had privately conversed with Eliot about her "double-consciousness."

The Lifted Veil stood out in the context of the parallels between George Eliot and me. I could better describe Eliot's "double-consciousness," as mentioned in her 1860 travel journal, by describing my own similar experiences. When I was a child, I would stand and look at something beautiful for a prolonged period of time, hoping to extract every detail for memory's sake: a crimson sunset, a patch of moss fetched-up in what appeared to be a fairy circle, or an acorn with its cap gone missing. I had always been good at imagery in poetry, perhaps because I was able to remember and weave together the details of things I'd seen years before as though looking at them for the first time while penning the words—just like Eliot.

But also like Eliot, I would lose the trail if I wasn't tuned in properly—focused on the original moment of observation and inspiration. It would seem that the details of things we wish to commit to memory are etched onto the mind's canvas through a heightened sense beyond the ordinary. For each of us, the past is recreated with great clarity in the present moment—"relived" so to speak.

I wondered if Eliot could project her consciousness into the future. Was she able to know Latimer as a character with double-consciousness because she possessed the same faculties? Though the story seemed enticing, I was stuck in the Introduction. The editor had done her work—sucked me into a place of no return.

In the opening paragraph of *The Lifted Veil*, the tone is set as an egocentric, clairvoyant named Latimer foretold his own death. He was able to read the minds of everyone but Bertha, his wife. She was not in charge of her mental and emotional faculties. Perhaps she lost her mind when Latimer's brother died before he and Bertha were to be wed. Latimer took up the business of making a home for Bertha by default.

The end of the novella reveals a doctor leaning over his dead patient, Latimer, administering a blood transfusion to stimulate revivification (bringing the dead patient back to life). The cadaver sprang to life, leaned forward in the bed and pointed at Bertha, marking her as the murderer! Latimer dropped back to the bed and died again, having delivered the secret from beyond death.

Norm and I chatted about *The Lifted Veil*. I still could not believe that Eliot entertained the same thoughts I was now entertaining. Norm set me straight on it, "Nothing's ever new, Freda. Old stories are rewritten into new stories. Emerson said, 'Before you begin to write, you begin to read.' We base what we know to be truth on what has gone before us, either to prove or disprove it and record the results. That's what literature is." My husband, the professor!

I enjoyed the metaphysical aspects of this novella. Eliot was unreserved in her opening paragraphs of *The Lifted Veil*. She let it rip right out of the gate. I was not surprised to learn that *The Lifted Veil* was more popular today than when it was written by the realist who had just pulled off her moral masterpiece, *Adam Bede*. This daring book was no *Adam Bede*—though Eliot did try to counter the fluffy books being shared by British ladies over tea. *The Lifted Veil* would have shocked them right out of their pantaloons!

-14-

Invisible

What could be more important than reading what makes you laugh, cry, and feel religious? I begged for mercy, but none came. "Are you watching this, George? This is all your fault," I said to no one there. After a period of anguish and a pound bar of chocolate, I undertook the task of reading a collection of essays and other writings from *George Eliot: Selected Critical Writings*, Oxford World's Classics edition. This collection provided rich commentary, revealing the likes and dislikes of the author.

George Eliot had diverse tastes in art, and in an excerpt from Chapter 17 of *Adam Bede*, she defended her common, and sometimes sinful, characters. Her point was that Adam Bede depicted the common in life: both the beauty and the beast of it. She could not apply "high church" characteristics to those who were mere mortals. Boom!

Eliot continued to develop her point of view for her readers by defending the Dutch painters for their honest simplicity of form. She could sympathize with the painters and their subjects rooted deeply in nature and the commonplace. Eliot expressed her love of rural England in many of her novels just as the Dutch painters had infused their love of the common into their paintings. I loved the work of Dutch painters too. My favorite artist, Johannes Vermeer, is perhaps the most famous of the Dutch painters. His paintings reveal a subtle quality of natural light in common settings.

Eliot admired the painters in the Brotherhood of the Pre-Raphaelites who shunned the Royal Academy in London. In art, as in many other areas of Eliot's life, she was a realist and didn't mind rebelling for the sake of those who had no voice. In *Adam Bede* she penned a passage about art, describing poetically the common folk displayed in the Dutch paintings. Eliot was well aware of the fact that the London elite despised the common in the Dutch paintings, nonetheless, she championed the Pre-Raphaelite painters through the common characters in her own novels.

As I read, I remembered that I had written many poems about the common. My poem, "Sugarcreek: for the Amish" was an "unconventional sonnet," as *Writer's Digest* had referred to it. Winning third place in an international contest, the poem brought me "The Outstanding Ohioan" award. Its beauty and simplicity made it shine like the light of a Vermeer painting.

Eliot's first publication was a poem in the evangelical vein published in *The Christian Observer* in 1840 when she was twenty years old. Coincidentally, my poems were first published in a newspaper when I was twenty two. She had always loved Wordsworth, and shared with him a joy for the English countryside. Wordsworth had long been one of my favorite poets. I fancied visiting his home one day in the Lake District of Grasmere, England. Eliot resented applying "form" to all poetry as well as art. Dante Gabriel Rosetti, William Morris and others squared with her views on writing and art for the masses.

One of Eliot's most famous poems, "O MAY I Join the Choir Invisible," shared an excerpt for her epitaph, "...of those immortal dead who live again in minds made better by their presence." The first line and first stanza are from a Methodist hymn. The poem's title and first line rang a bell with me. I searched in the poetry I'd written to find the poem that, in my memory, seemed similar. It was a simple free verse poem titled "Harmony" and the introductory quote for the poem was by Don Costello, "There is a choir loft in the soul...." Eliot's poem is also introduced by a quote. Both of our poems are speaking of the goodness men leave behind for mankind through their soul work. In this way, Eliot believed, we are immortal—remaining in the minds and hearts of men. Both poems appear in Appendix B of this book.

Suddenly I was reminded of another literary similarity between Eliot and me. While reading *The Mill on the Floss*, I had noticed in the opening paragraph of the first chapter that Eliot had mentioned willow trees while sharing a reminiscence about the old days back at Dorlcote Mill: "I remember those large dipping willows," she said. I had written a poem titled "Willows"—reminiscing about the old days at our farm. I thumbed through my poetry collection again, and found the one that was nearly the same in word and meaning to that of Eliot's passage. Another coincidence? "I remember willows bending toward ground—dipping, swaying—pendulums sweeping time."

In addition, there were references in Eliot's writings about the common appearance of hay ricks and sheaves punctuating the English countryside. My writing is steeped in the same nostalgia of rural Ohio—icons of a simple life. My landscape and her landscape were nearly the same.

Eliot and I shared the love of the common in life—the goodness that comes by honest work and the shouldering of adversities. We both valued individuality—the free thinker, the autonomous ways and means that make each person a god so to speak.

In our creative efforts in art, literature, and music there were incredible similarities between us. I almost felt as though Eliot bade me to listen to Haydn, Liszt, and

Wagner—opened my eyes to recognize the genius of the Pre-Raphaelite painters—guided my pen to write the striking imagery and metaphors that seemed eerily similar to her own. Two could not have resonated more than Eliot and I did in the area of the arts. But she was the master; I was the student sitting at her feet watching her glassy gray eyes as she shared her life in incremental stories through me.

Part 3

∞ Unleashing the Lunacy ∞

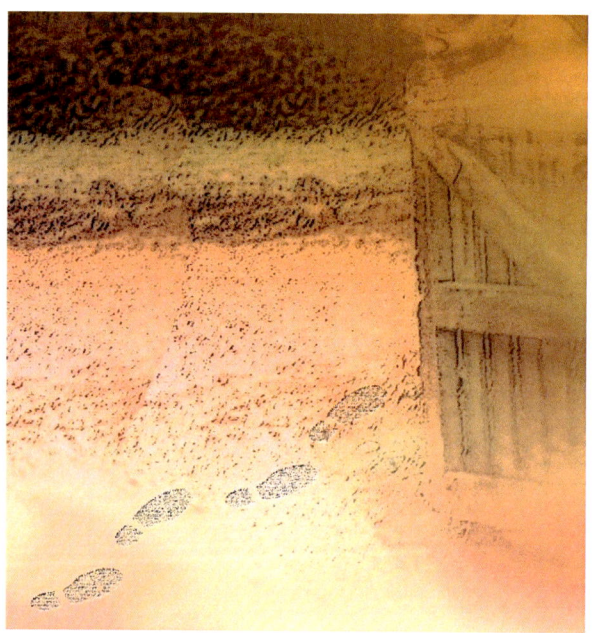

–15–

Cinderella

Eliot and I were both vulnerable in our own ways. She was self-conscious about her looks, but she more than made up for her lack of beauty with her brilliant mind. I was a bit less concerned about my looks, and was by no stretch of the imagination, brilliant. But I was creative, innovative, and tenacious—the turtle in the story of the turtle and the hare.

Both Eliot and I played the Cinderella role dutifully. Though she worked unceasingly to care for her father until his death, she gained no honor for her devotion. I knew that feeling even though I had not been my father's caretaker. It was the feeling of being no one's princess. I realize now that he always loved his children, but he did not know how to express it when we were growing up. I think that part of him may have passed with my mother. As a child, I felt he kept me as a duty—a commitment to my mother to keep her children together and take care of them until she could see them again in heaven. There was no way to live up to the image of my mother's ghost—she was gone, and she was perfect—incorruptible. I spent my formative years trying to gain my father's love and acceptance. I carried the psychological scars through my childhood years and well into my adult years, watching my relationships fail because I tried too hard to please people even if they'd done nothing to earn my trust or love.

A few times during my childhood, my stepmother ran away from my father, later citing various grievances. For brief periods of time I was left managing the household for my father and two older brothers. A specific memory lingers in my mind about one of those times. I was in the cool farm kitchen near the white porcelain sink. I stood looking into the groaning Frigidaire full of milk, homemade butter, cherry jelly, some leftover spaghetti, and two pitchers—one full of Kool Aid and the other iced tea. I knelt down peering deep into the low, dark shelves searching for something to make for my father's lunch. In my apron, I scooped up a carton of eggs, mustard, mayonnaise, onions, and a loaf of sliced bread. I proceeded to make egg salad for sandwiches. My father carried his lunch off to work without a word. The coffee I had prepared for him that morning resembled mud. I knew I had been a great disappointment instead of a comfort in his time of need.

Trying to make up for my lack of kitchen skills, I cracked some black walnuts we'd stored from the previous year. My hands were stained and hurting, but in spite of all obstacles,

I managed to produce a handful of black walnuts, my father's favorite. I used the nutmeats to make cookies, adding them in proudly. My father ate them without his usual waving of hands and rolling of eyes. He said nothing. He was hurting, but so was I. Somehow he couldn't relate to what was hurting his children because he was busy with work or steeped in his own emotional pain. Along with the memories, came tears. I wondered how many times Eliot, as an adult, had done the same—tried to please her father to no avail. Norm had grown accustomed to my "Cinderella moments" when I wept over something my family said or did to make me feel inadequate.

I could not blame my family. I simply had to accept what was, learn more coping skills, and move on. Eliot would call this kind of coping, "duty." I would call this "overcoming negative karma." If I could do the Buddha thing, apply a few of "The Four Noble Truths," I could shift my mood and my karma all at once. "Life is full of suffering." Yes, it is. "Suffering is caused by attachment, greed, or desire." I agree with that. "Suffering ends when we see the impermanence of everything." All is impermanent—we live, we die, we are reborn to begin the cycle anew. The only sure thing in life was change—change was permanent! As long as change was inevitable, I would pray for easy transitions.

Norm warned me that I should take a break from Eliot. "You are dragging yourself down," he said. He had a tendency to abbreviate his sentences when he was nervous. Next came the pursing of his lips and the twitching of his nose. The final phase, when there was nothing else to be said or done, was the removal of his glasses, followed by a methodical rubbing of the space between his caterpillar eyebrows.

It was true; I was driven to learn more about Eliot—to see what she had for me. I was being washed over by memories so vivid they might have happened yesterday. I was taking on Eliot's pain on top of my own. My husband was feeling bad for me, even though he couldn't empathize, he could sympathize. He was the eldest son of a family who adored him. How could he know how it felt to be separated from family? How could he know the pain of reviewing the long decades of hurt that had settled somewhere in the base of my spine and clawed its way up to my mind? But Norm was right, I was spending too much time on Eliot—giving her pain too many chances to leech into my own life.

A walk would help me clear my head. Nature had a way of resetting my rudder, of adjusting my sail for the reception of a clean and purifying wind. I stepped outdoors to find the manor house was surrounded by a mist rising up from the steaming soil. It sent chills through me! There was a sense of "otherness." But I had always felt that otherness—defining it as God, or mother, or guardian angels. *Was it Eliot all along? Was it her lingering sense of duty vested into my life?* Perhaps she was trying to help me, this other Cinderella soul, to get beyond what she, in her final years, championed in her own life.

I found a patch of moss with a few wildflowers springing from its center. I brushed my hand over it lightly, remembering the fairy cushions of my childhood. My footsteps startled a rabbit nearby. It ran into a thicket surrounded by honeysuckle vines—a sweet shelter. Rabbits were the easiest prey, out in the middle of nowhere with only speed to save them. A well-placed thicket here and there assured survival of the hare in rural areas. We had many thickets because I insisted that Norm leave them undisturbed.

The pond wore patches of algae, and cattails closed in the perimeter. I peered across the water and saw the broken willow tree still struggling to push forth minnow-shaped leaves, its bark as old as the town of Mount Vernon, its roots as deep as the family sod from which it sprang. Suddenly, it seemed as though Eliot was there—there beside me, just as she had stood beside the small pond near the Griff House where she and her brother fished when they were children.

True epiphany moments were rare, but this was one that was a sure scene penned by Eliot as the narrator in *The Mill on the Floss:*

Nature repairs her ravages—but not all. The uptorn trees are not rooted again; the parted hills are left scarred: if there is new growth, the trees are not the same as the old, and the hills underneath their green vesture bear the marks of the past rending. To the eyes that have dwelt on the past, there is no thorough repair.

It was almost as though she were reading the lines to me from the conclusion of her book. Her images were hauntingly real for my own Cinderella life.

The great blue heron glided by as though a ship on calm water. I walked where it flew its charted course, aligning my spirit with that of the heron. Gliding over the dew-damp grass, feeling a sudden lightness of head—almost levitation, but my feet were firmly planted. Undoubtedly, my thoughts were moving out beyond me demonstrating the law of attraction. The Universe, God, Mother, Angel, Eliot— whoever was receiving my signals at just that moment were responding with new, fresh energy!

Did the heron know she had left a wake for me to follow? Did she have her course charted long ago, knowing someday she would put down at our pond and find it satisfying, setting her preened feathers back in order, stepping high in the cover of the cattails?

I walked on with a sudden new sense of purpose. I had been visited by something—someone, like a Cinderella moment when the fairy godmother finds her at her lowest ebb, weeping at the dark hearth—the energy of that moment creating limitless possibilities for change, for evolution, for new karmic imprints.

I needed to get on with the duty of writing *the* book—to give meaning to this *current* life's experience—this pain which sorts its way out of a stack of aging first editions to serve as a beacon of hope for others. That's what Eliot did, and that's what I would do! I ran toward the house, boots flinging mud as I went. Sadie was pacing behind me. "That's it!" I declared to myself. Eliot's life was *not* a complete story, and mine may not complete the story either. But I would write my version!

I saw Norm waiting for me by the kitchen door. His thick gray hair was tousled, giving him a devil-may-care appearance. Perhaps he'd been pondering a change of hairstyle after seeing the lovely portrait of Byron under vellum. I ran by, leaving him with his mouth hanging open and a look of confusion on his face. Poor man—to be married to a driven woman like me—a writer with the gumption of Eliot. George and I would sort this out together.

–16–

Mentors

I was on a natural high! My words were flowing to paper in true Eliot fashion. Soon a neat pile of 8 ½ by 11 sheets lay on my maple desktop. Over the next several months, I would be bent over my computer keyboard tapping out messages to myself as part of the process of learning who I am, why I am here, and how Eliot played into my story.

I wrote again to Dr. Heinemann. He would be shocked by the latest developments in the continuing Eliot saga. In the note, I explained to him that I was writing *the* book, and that I had selected a working title. I shared my most recent findings with him, and wished him and his wife well. Then back to work I went, unwinding the word ribbons between Eliot and me. The more I read, the more I intuited her subtle meanings. And then there were times when Eliot was anything but subtle—as though she were marching across the floor of my office with her head thrown back and her gray eyes flashing with ideas. I loved those moments because she reminded me that she could be spunky like me. She was great company at the keyboard.

The more I worked, the more I sensed many mentors. Among them were Norm, Dr. Heinemann and his wife Gundi; George Eliot and her soul mate, Lewes, who seemed to be synced to Eliot's interaction with me; Emerson who spoke volumes to me as I typed; Goethe who chimed in to confuse me with his guttural German accent; Emily Dickinson shyly resting in the shadows offering up a metaphor or two; Harriet Beecher Stowe leaning in to offer wisdom; and Henry James—oh dear Henry, the literary critic who thought *Middlemarch* was contrived compared to Eliot's early novel plots. These, all, were mentors marching down a long literary line to stand behind me at my modest desk, offering advice, fussing with one another about the content, grammar, and punctuation. So real was their presence that I could almost hear their voices chattering in one ear, and then the other. It was almost a scene from the movie, *Miss Potter,* where Peter Rabbit thumped his leg to get Beatrix's attention, then kicked up dust making his way out of Mr. McGregor's garden. Beatrix Potter befriended her creations, and I was befriending those who had created before me, weaving them into the tender story of my life—my life of literary lunacy!

That evening, after a simple supper of roasted stuffed peppers, I took email messages before starting back to work on my book. My daughter, Vicki, had written, sharing some pictures of her "baby belly" as she called it. She was to give birth in December, and I was thrilled knowing it would be a girl this time. Another email popped in from a prayer line, and finally a congratulatory email from Dr. Heinemann. He always wrote his emails in yellow stationery background, twelve point type, Arial font. He knew what worked best for him and stuck with it, much the same way Casaubon—I mean Norm—did. Dr. Heinemann's note began by saying he and Mrs. Heinemann had finalized some stories for their book, and had made contact with a fascinating gentleman who photographed orbs with a camera lens intact. That I would have to see to believe! He added that his agent had taken his book proposal to the Frankfurt Book Fair in Germany. Hay House and two other prominent publishers had bid on his book. He wished me well on my own venture, and looked forward to reading some of my chapters soon. I felt honored to be featured in the Heinemann's book, *Orbs: Their Mission and Messages of Hope*. Even though the book was not my own, it made me feel confident about publishing my full story someday. It always felt good to hear from the Heinemanns—something about their confident manner kept me moving forward.

Within days, Klaus wrote to me again, saying that the negotiations with his agent were at a standstill, and he and his wife were scheduled to leave the country. I asked if I could be of assistance by working with the agent while they were away. My offer was accepted, and I emailed his agent asking if I could be of any help while the Heinemanns were away. I explained to her that I had edited *Orbs*, and that the abbreviated version of my story, *The Mill on the Floss Project*, was in the book. She wrote back to say that she was working diligently on getting the bids in for all three publishers, but that one of them would likely opt out if they were outbid on the next round.

Within hours, the agent wrote to say that the book had a publisher. I contacted Klaus. He was adamant that their preferred publisher be brought back to the table. For them, it wasn't about the largest advance, but who could get the books on the most shelves and keep them there. We all worked together to bring results. Klaus emailed to suggest we celebrate with a phone call. For the first time, I heard his German accent as he answered the phone.

"Klaus here!" He sounded like the Goethe mentor of my writing imagination!

"Hello, Klaus, George Eliot here!" At first there was a pause, then he remembered my association with George Eliot.

"Oh, yes, yes, right! How are you?"

"I'm fine, and so is Norm. We are excited for you and Gundi. Congratulations!"

"Yes, yes, and you must be too! Thank you for all of your help in editing, for your intriguing story for our book, and for your assistance with communicating with our agent. I will call my agent next to follow up on the email news from her."

"You are most welcome, Klaus. It has been the adventure of a lifetime for me. I will let you go so that you can prepare for your call. Good to talk with you, and blessings to you both."

"Yes, yes, goodbye then." There was a click at the other end, and Klaus was gone. I had just talked with the man who had expanded my consciousness, and moved me forward with my own book of self-discovery. It was pleasing to assist the UK agent on behalf of the Heinemanns. It was the least I could do after Klaus and Gundi's time and energy investment into *The Mill on the Floss* Project.

The manuscript on my desk was getting thicker, and soon I had several chapters. I sent them to Klaus for an initial reading. I also sent them to a friend of mine who owned a literary and film production company in Hollywood. The Heinemanns loved the story, and it brought encouraging comments from my Hollywood friend as well. I felt confident enough to move forward with my book.

It never ceased to amaze me that the simple sketch of my life was being juxtaposed with the grand portrait of Eliot's.

As Norm and I shared my writings, I jokingly dubbed myself "Georgy," and sang the Seeker's song "Georgy Girl" around the house until I drove us both crazy with it. We had great fun reading my manuscript as I pretended to be sharing with George Lewes, Eliot's soulmate. In written correspondence, Norm referred to me as his "Mary Ann." I found it interesting that he made that distinction. Perhaps he believed, as did I, that the pattern of my life seemed to fit into the template of Eliot's early life at Griff.

Systematically, I tied together the threads of our lives and correspondences, our likes and dislikes, what influenced our thoughts as we matured. Most of Eliot's mentors were men, and an ideal day for her was a day spent behind closed doors with her soulmate, George Lewes, sharing philosophical thoughts and literary ramblings. Lewes' lack of beauty was insignificant to George Eliot. She was completely satisfied with "the ugliest man in London" as his friend, Douglas Jerrold called him. Even this was a bit better than Thomas Carlyle's description of George Lewes when he called him, "Ape." Finding such comments in Marghanita Laski's book brought a grin to my face. Even though Lewes was unable to divorce his first wife, Agnes, and even though he was not handsome, he and Eliot were perfect partners in every way. George Eliot brought her own baggage and less than lovely appearance to the relationship, but their commonalities fused them in literary love and companionship.

Like Eliot, I enjoyed the company of men. Perhaps it was a natural inclination since I had grown up with two older brothers while being fairly isolated from female peers. That preference worked for Norm. He needed a buddy he could feel comfortable with—someone with whom he could read and share ideas. And he thought it fascinating that I could figure out a mechanical problem on the car before he could! I could stand toe-to-toe with seasoned farmers, businessmen, contractors, city council, and even Norm. On the weekends, we spent our time together enjoying movies, concerts, and bookstores. Sometimes just taking a nature walk together was an adventure. It didn't matter what others thought, we were perfect partners just as Eliot and Lewes had been.

Neither Norm nor I were steady in religion or church-going. But we were both steady in our empathy and our love for mankind, especially those who were less fortunate. Both of our lives had been shaped by spending time with "salt of the earth" characters from small towns and farming communities. I have a vivid memory of a time in high school when a popular girl told me I should stop hanging around with a certain unsavory character because she would surely ruin my reputation. My heart spoke louder than the misguided advice, and I continued my friendship with the girl who stood alone at recess watching the would-be debutantes with their perfectly coiffed hair circle like

Piranha beyond her social reach. It would not be the first or the last time I stepped out in compassion.

Norm and I had both slipped from social graces in high school. But *he* weathered it brilliantly! As a young adult, he loved words so much that he strung copper wires across his bedroom to hang vocabulary words he wanted to learn. When I was young, I dragged through second-hand books at yard sales to find dictionaries and vocabulary primers. We were destined to be together. My teachers were my mentors as well as a handful of concerned folks along the way. I met most of my mentors, my ordinary heroes, in the process of earning money selling monogrammed greeting cards and *Grit* newspaper. Norm had a paper route too. This was our way of getting beyond our home boundaries—to see how others were living their lives.

According to Norm, he was overly-protected in his childhood. Me—not so much. Oddly, we both grew up requiring certain freedoms. I was independent because it was required of me as a child. "Get off your lazy rump, and do it yourself!" my stepmother would say. Norm was independent because he resisted being monitored by family. Hillary Clinton said, "It takes a village," but in reality, it takes a lifetime—perhaps several lifetimes of mentors, guides, friends, and family to make us who we are meant to be: members in a soul group of students who revisit the situations that help them grow.

Our ancestors with whom we share history are part of us— part of the great puzzle of our soul evolution. Perhaps Robert Evans' family and my maternal Evans family *were* remotely related. To date, I'd found no evidence of that. But I had played with numbers to learn that there were approximately seventy three years (or three generations) between Eliot's death and my birth. Between the time Eliot began a serious relationship with George Lewes, in 1853, and the year that I was born, 1953, counted one hundred years almost to the month! The soulmates referred to that fateful coming together as a "rebirth."

Another synchronicity I discovered while researching family records was that my paternal Aunt Freda, for whom I am a namesake, shared a birthday with George Eliot. Aunt Freda was stillborn on November 22. We are all walking a timeline, experiencing recurring time cycles here on the Earth plane. Gregg Braden talks about this in his book, *Fractal Time*. Nothing short of remarkable!

Freda M. Chaney

-17-

Reincarnation

I was spent! I'd worn myself out thinking, researching, writing, making trips to the library and bookstores. In addition, I was still caring for Norm, bed and breakfast guests, the house and gardens, and trying to squeeze in time to see my daughter and grandson. *Friends? Did I still have friends?* I felt like Eliot, secluded in her upstairs room forcing herself to write while her head ached like nobody's business. I had sick headaches almost daily. They came with the territory of writing. Perhaps I was straining my eyes from reading books and editing manuscripts, or maybe it had something to do with the angle of my neck as I was writing. The stress of not knowing if one's book would be a success could be a big factor in constant headaches. No matter, Eliot and I wrote anyway.

"You just need a break," Norm said. "You'll see. Once you get this book published, the others will follow." Norm was right. I was used to rejection slips from agents and publishers, and I had long since learned to tuck my pride. I just had to stick with it, and do my best. It was good to have a mate who worked with me and not against me. For Eliot, it took the support of George Lewes, and the subsequent success of *Adam Bede* to convince her that she was capable of writing novels. Nothing she set her pen to thereafter failed to generate public appreciation.

I'd have to don the hide of Eliot. She set her mind to creating that which would express the deepest concerns of her time period as well as the perennial questions of love and morality. Somehow, her wisdom leaped from the page into her readers' lives. Whether people loved her or hated her, they bought her work. She said what most needed to be said even in the face of rejection. She had already been rejected by society, by family, and many of her friends. Perhaps this gave her the freedom she needed to be the sage of early women's fiction.

Her writing reputation had stood the test of time. Modern women were returning to their college editions to see how their mature lives echoed the characters in Eliot's books. The young readers were just discovering Eliot and juxtaposing her life and writings with Jane Austen for some dusty classroom exercise. But there was nothing dusty about George Eliot! The youthful readers would find in her the same free-thinking spirit they possessed, a touch of rebellion—though leveraged in an intelligent way. She was spirited and a bit sassy. Younger generations would like that!

Norm was going out the door with his little black doctor's bag that he'd found years ago. The latch on the top was broken, and the case was showing much wear, but he carried it everywhere he went. It held books, pens and pencils, a pad of paper, a cell phone, and snacks. He always carried a stash of sweets to keep his energy up. Norm was a man who wouldn't be stopped. He went methodically about his business, but he went when and where others would not. Today, his travels would take him three hundred miles to visit with his mother, and three hundred miles back home to Ohio.

I watched my husband walk down the sidewalk past the obelisk and Saint Francis statue. Norm's straight backbone and determined step revealed his Scottish ancestry. When Norm disappeared around the corner of the garage, I peered down toward the footbridge at the pond. I could see apples on the gnarled tree. Though we had a young orchard near the pond, this particular tree bore the best tasting fruit. It is fabled to have been planted by John Chapman, also known as Johnny Appleseed, when the town of Mount Vernon was young. John Chapman owned property in Mount Vernon, and his sister lived in the town as well. He would stay with her when he was in the area, sharing his apple seeds and spreading the gospel of Emanuel Swedenborg. Everything about our property seemed sacred, like a miniature Findhorn in Ohio. The gnarled apple tree was well acclimated to the area and kept right on bearing fruit even though its trunk was nearly hollow.

I had to stay home to watch over the house, the dog, and the stray cats, but this time I didn't mind. The quiet space gave me plenty of room to do research and writing. It was just this kind of relationship that existed between George Eliot and her soulmate, George Lewes. Eliot wrote in her office while Lewes made social connections and ran errands for them. She was content to be at home the same as I. Still, it would be a long weekend without Norm. I would stick my head into books and read for days, not leaving the house unless it was necessary. I stepped back from the doorway and resolved to get some satisfactory research done on day one of his absence. My cozy office was calling as my mind rambled into a thousand spaces and places it wanted to go. But the act of creation required my focus and commitment. I'd get there if it killed me.

I remember a movie I'd watched many years ago, *Field of Dreams*, about a man who was about to lose the family farm. He started hearing a voice in his head urging him to create a baseball field. He was confused about what it could mean, but he continued to listen to the inner voice. With his wife's encouragement, he built the baseball field. But who would play? They had no way of getting a big game together out in the middle of an Iowa cornfield! Because the farmer dared to dream, and courageously stepped out to begin the creation process, the Universe opened to him and answered the desires of his heart. Soon, a uniformed cast of famous, but ghostly, characters from baseball's history magically appeared on the field to play ball. People filled the field to watch the game, and the money for the tickets paid off the family farm.

There were so many books I could reference in relation to the theme of *Field of Dreams*. For instance, *The Celestine Prophecy* and its sequel *The Tenth Insight* by James Redfield. The author wrote these fictional accounts to show that the Universe is alive—awaiting the input of our desires, dreams, wishes, hopes, commands. We humans are linked with the Universe, and the Universe with us. What's more, we are linked together as spirits living out our lives in flesh suits. All of these interconnections, according to Redfield create a streaming Universe full of possibilities.

Gregg Braden speaks of the same Universe of possibilities in many of his books. In *The God Code*, Braden shares this concept through a divinely imprinted DNA in humans. The conscious being is connected to the Divine through a purposeful creation and sharing of DNA at a cellular energy level. Humans are connected to one another in this way, as are animals. We are a connected web of energy interaction— a matrix if you will—with God as designer.

These insights leave much to ponder about our abilities to create our own world. First, they indicate that we, as divine beings, are in charge of our decisions, our lives, and yes, our repeated lives if we don't learn the lessons each lifetime offers. They also reveal that we affect others' lives. We live on this planet to make a difference in the lives of others in relation to ourselves. The writings of authors such as Gregg Braden and James Redfield reveal that our connections can cause great reverberations within our world. It is mind-boggling to realize that the divine soul can attract what it needs, create its world, live there to interact with others and learn life lessons, leave the physical world through the death of the body, and be reborn to begin the creation cycle anew. The "law of attraction" and "manifestation" are two of the most compelling topics on the metaphysical book market today. No longer are such books just for New Age readers.

Books about reincarnation, past lives, and parallel lives are also on the same popularity bookshelf. According to a *New York Times* article by Lisa Miller in 2010 titled "Remembrances of Times Past," she reports her findings from data released by the Pew Forum on Religion and Public Health. The data indicates that one fourth of all Americans believe in reincarnation.

Where "New Agers" may have revived the ancient spiritual thoughts (including those of Jesus) about reincarnation, we now have scientists on board, opening the dusty doors for modern man to take a "rational" look at reincarnation in a new light.

I was familiar with the work of Edgar Cayce so I perused the shelves to see if I could locate a book by "the sleeping prophet." I found two immediately. One was a hardbound with the title *Edgar Cayce, Modern Prophet* by Mary Ellen Carter under the direction of Hugh Lynn Cayce, Edgar's son. It contained four volumes under one cover. In the "Conclusion" of book four, reincarnation is called a "code of ethics" not a theory as many propose. The text goes on to say this about reincarnation:

> It was an essential part of the early Gospels, and its removal...has never been satisfactorily accounted for. Scattered references to it still exist in the Bible, but the encyclopedias have been steadily diminishing their emphasis on it since 1911—the last edition of the *Encyclopedia Britannica* to deal frankly with it under the heading Metempsychosis.

> Edgar Cayce's readings accept it [reincarnation] unequivocally, and repeatedly insist that positive and negative conduct in earlier lives actively affect behavior patterns in the present. That which is negative can be resolved and overcome, once a man is

prepared to accept his problems as being entirely of his own making, and therefore responsive to his un-making.

The other book, *Edgar Cayce, An American Prophet*, by Sidney Kirkpatrick, offered equally intriguing information regarding reincarnation, but something drew me specifically to "The Life of Christ." Ah, yes, the chapter title was similar to the title of the book Eliot translated into English in 1846, Strauss' *Das Leben Jesu. (The Life of Jesus)*. In a particular reading, Cayce was given information by the "Source" about how the way was prepared for the birth of Christ. Kirkpatrick wrote,

> In a particularly fascinating discourse on biblical history, the Source suggested that preparations for the coming of the Messiah were underway for four hundred years before the birth of Jesus. According to Cayce, the people who were "preparing the way," and in whose midst Jesus was eventually born, were the Essenes, or the "Brotherhood." Cayce described them as "a [non-celibate] religious order within Jewry," whose primary function was as record keepers, interpreters of prophecy, and channels for the Messiah to come. According to the readings, because of their belief in astrology, numerology, and

reincarnation, they were also generally viewed by the greater Jewish population as rebels and radicals.

For modern historians, the Essenes have long been an enigma, primarily because there is little mention of the sect's existence after the birth of Jesus. Much of what is now known about the Essenes comes from the Dead Sea Scrolls, which were discovered in Qumran in 1947, more than a decade after Cayce first discussed the Essenes and two years after his death.

What if the lineage of Jesus, according to the Dead Sea Scrolls and according to Cayce's Source, was through the Essenes who practiced what we term in the modern world as New Age principles? Mary Ann might have asked herself the same questions after reading controversial literature given to her by the Brays and Hennells at Rosehill. It brought doubts to her mind regarding the commonly accepted Jesus she had worshiped from an early age. She was learning about a more human Jesus who may have been largely influenced by the Essenes. This Jesus made more sense to a young woman who had entered a new social setting of intellectual friends in Coventry, daring to ask bold questions and seek answers no matter the risks. Mary Ann was no longer the evangelical that poured her devoted heart and soul out to her mentor, Miss Lewis. Rather, she was the open-minded Miss

Evans, a "new thinker" among other intellectuals who were soaking up philosophy like sponges.

I had followed the same path as young Mary Ann, reading the Bible and going to Bible study at the neighbor's house as a young girl. I struggled with church-going in my twenties, but eventually returned to the fold in my thirties. I taught my daughter and foster children everything I knew, and we kept churched-up three days a week. It was our way of life.

My way of life and thoughts about Jesus began to change when I was in my forties, after I married Norm. He was an Elder in a mainstream Protestant church, but like Mary Ann, Norm also had an open mind. After numerous heated conversations where I stood my ground like the most devoted disciple, Norm convinced me to look into the history of Christianity. I was drawn to the study of the Essenes as Mary Ann had been.

Another interesting thing I learned was that the Magi who followed the star of Bethlehem to find the baby Jesus were not just Wise Men or Kings of the Orient, but astrologers said to have psychic powers and visions. According to biblical accounts and other ancient texts that were left out of the Bible, Jesus had many of these same attributes and then some. Moreover, prophets from the Old Testament had visions and dreamed prophetic dreams.

In my earlier readings from *Edgar Cayce Modern Prophet*, a paragraph stood out on the page with a quote from Dr. Weatherhead:

> One wonders why men have so readily accepted the idea of a life after death, and so largely in the West, discarded the idea of a life before birth. So many arguments for a one-way immortality seem to me cogent for a two-way life outside the present body.

While the Buddhists and Hindus declare reincarnation openly, many Jews and Christians traditionally do not. They affirm there is life after death, but not life before birth. Yet, there are passages in the Bible where the idea of reincarnation seems to be hinted at, if not acknowledged, as in the parable that Jesus tells in Luke 16 of the rich man who wants Abraham to send Lazarus to speak to his brothers and save them from the torments of hell. The rich man pleaded, "...if one went unto them from the dead, they will repent." Abraham answered him, "If they hear not Moses and the prophets, neither will they be persuaded, though one rose from the dead." (Luke 16:30-31 *King James Version*). *Does the parable suggest a recycling of the soul from life to death, from death to life? Is there more to the thought life of Jesus than the Bible records indicate? Is that thought life related to the Essenes?* These are questions that I cannot answer. But I sense these questions are similar to those Eliot might have asked herself when she was drifting away from the strict religious teachings of her youth.

Drawing primarily from the Hindu tradition, the Bhagavad Gita (Song of God) is a summary of Eastern spiritual wisdom. To simplify, it speaks of Krishna as God within man. This text was introduced to America and caught on with a fervor in Concord where Thoreau, Emerson, Alcott, Whitman, and others in the Transcendentalist movement valued it highly. Emerson had one of the first volumes in the States, and loaned it to others. Europe had already been saturated with Eastern thought. But in reading a passage in *Reincarnation: The Phoenix Fire Mystery*, I learned that the Theosophists introduced the Bhagavad Gita to Ghandi! Theosophists used mystical insight to understand the nature of God, and fully embraced the Bhagavad Gita. It seemed that the Bhagavad Gita had come full circle from the East to the West and back again.

I studied religion to earn my degree in divinity, but was I ready for personal proof of reincarnation? I wondered if my knowledge of Eliot was opening my eyes to new spiritual truths. Could the spiritual knowledge she obtained after she met the Brays be similar to the information I was now reading? Eliot had been influenced by Immanuel Kant's philosophy, as well as by Goethe, Blake, Emerson and others. I felt like a freed bird while reading Emerson and other

Transcendentalists in the 1970s, and Norm introduced me to Goethe in the 1990s. In between, I had questions, but no real answers. The lotus flower was opening.

Thoreau left much evidence on his views of reincarnation. As I was reading *Reincarnation: The Phoenix Fire Mystery*, I found an excerpt from one of Thoreau's letters to a spiritual disciple, Harrison Blake, dated April 3, 1850. Thoreau wrote, "I lived in Judea eighteen hundred years ago, but I never knew that there was such a one as Christ among my contemporaries." And in another excerpt from a letter to Blake on February 27, 1853, he wrote, "As the stars looked to me when I was a shepherd in Assyria, they look to me now a New Englander." Also in *Reincarnation: The Phoenix Fire Mystery*, I found a passage taken from Thoreau's journals, from July 16, 1851. "As far back as I can remember I have unconsciously referred to the experiences of a previous state of existence."

Oh, Thoreau! His words were brief—to the point, but his message was huge. He made an indelible mark on generations of thinkers. His esteemed friend, Ralph Waldo Emerson, shared regular conversations with him. Thoreau was a helper around the Emerson home. I could see their influence on one another in their philosophical renderings. I believe Thoreau's message is just as strong in our modern times as it was in the 1800s.

Emerson was the formative thinker of Transcendentalism who shared his vision broadly both in essays and lectures. He had a loyal friend and ally in Amos Bronson Alcott who, no doubt, had influenced Emerson's thinking. As a teacher, Alcott openly taught principles of reincarnation at his Temple School in Boston, though the school was short-lived. Emerson was an avid supporter of Alcott's long-held dream to found a school of philosophy in Concord. That dream became a reality when Alcott opened the Concord Summer School of Philosophy at Orchard House. Many in Concord thought the school would not last, but it did. It was quite successful in bringing new thinkers to speak and teach within its walls. Among them were, William James, Julia Ward Howe, Elizabeth Peabody, and Emerson, the pride of Concord and Boston (see Louisamayalcott.org/csp/index). Not all of Alcott's ventures were successful. Some made him look downright silly to his peers. Fruitlands, the Utopian commune and agrarian experiment, had failed miserably. His failures aside, Amos Bronson Alcott applied his convictions to his daily life—lived them outwardly. Eliot and I could identify with that.

Norm would appreciate that Alcott, lesser known than Emerson, had an honorable place in *Reincarnation: The Phoenix Fire Mystery.* He had almost as many index entries as Thoreau, and a third as many as Emerson. I could see the three of them in my mind walking to Walden Pond, or gathering at the "philosopher's rock" behind the Old Manse. Dion's 1968 folk rock song, "Abraham, Martin, and John," came to mind. A songwriter somewhere must have written a song about these three Transcendentalists, hands clasped behind their backs, nodding their heads, exchanging quizzical looks, and all was well in Concord.

In Emerson's *Journals* of 1830, he wrote,

> The soul is an emanation of the Divinity, a part of the soul of the world, a ray from the source of light. It comes from without into the human body, as into a temporary abode, it goes out of it anew; it wanders in ethereal regions, it returns to visit...it passes into other habitations, for the soul is immortal.

Another entry from Emerson's *Journals* of 1843 stated, "...I know well that he builds no new world but by tearing down the old for materials." These words sank soul-deep for me. Yet, why were Emerson and Thoreau so sure that reincarnation was "truth?" While I could not answer that question directly, I trusted these icons of Transcendentalism today as I had trusted them in high school when I first came upon their cameos in our senior American Literature textbook. I had no doubt of Eliot's connection with the Transcendentalists who revered the Bhagavad Gita, but I wanted a deeper look into her world which guided her thoughts about Jesus in connection with Eastern thought.

Mary Ann (then twenty two years old) was first exposed to "new thinking" about Jesus' connection to the Jewish sect, the Essenes, through the Brays of Rosehill. They introduced her to the controversial publication, *An Inquiry Concerning the Origin of Christianity* written in 1838 by Charles Hennell, Charles Bray's brother-in-law. Shortly thereafter in 1842, she announced to her father that she could no longer attend church. Bray and Hennell had introduced questions about the miracles of Jesus, and the origin of Christian teachings. Mary Ann would be forever changed when she saw that Jesus' teachings reflected those of the Essenes who were influenced by Egyptian and Indian thought. The Essenes believed in reincarnation and karma.

Eliot became fascinated by Eastern thought that had already infiltrated Europe by the time she had her appetite whetted at Rosehill in 1841. Had she lived in the twentieth century, Eliot would have embraced the Dead Sea Scrolls and studied them to learn more about the Essenes and their connection with Jesus, but she might not have been so keen on Edgar Cayce's readings which shared the connection before the scrolls were discovered.

Cayce had his Source, but not everyone would trust his readings. His Source shared with him in dreams that he was to build a hospital where the work of Cayce could be used to heal patients. Cayce was fearful to forge ahead on his own, and asked many questions, relying on the Source, his friends, and benefactors to bring about the building of the learning center. He built the hospital before he knew that it would be a success. Just like the protagonist in the movie, *Field of Dreams,* Cayce dared to test the idea long before such law of attraction ideas were common conversation. Incredibly, the stock market crash of 1929 closed the hospital after only two years. But Cayce went on to do his work without the building. The original building for the Cayce Hospital in Virginia Beach now serves as the headquarters for the Association of Research and Enlightenment, a worldwide institution based on Edgar Cayce's life work.

I'd done the same thing with our home. I followed the urging of a dream, and did not rest fully until the dream was mine. At the first moment I saw our manor house high on a hill, I knew that it was perfect for us. For days on end, I designed orchards, and statuary gardens, created a library and book barn, planted an orchard and lived out days and nights—on paper. All of it now existed on our 5.9 acres in Knox County. Maybe I'd been given a vision of our home in advance. Someone *had* visited me in my dream. Were they telling me the house was mine—not to give up? Perhaps the actions of drawing the home and its surrounding acreage was a visual that prompted the Universe into creation. Had all of this been a grand design for George Eliot to get through to me and share wisdom about a previous life? Why would she follow me to impose her immortal message? *She didn't need me, or did she?*

The phone rang. I didn't want distractions just then. I looked at the caller ID and saw that it was Norm calling from Indiana. That was a distraction I did want. I picked up the receiver, "Hello, dear!"

"How are you? What are you doing?"

"Good! I've been doing some research on Edgar Cayce and the Dead Sea Scrolls."

"What got you on that track and off of Eliot?"

"Oh, it's the same track. At least I believe that to be the case. I started writing a chapter on how the Universe opens to us if we state our desires and work toward them. I threw in a bit of Redfield and Braden, and then made a natural turn to Edgar Cayce who learned through his Source."

"What source?" Norm interrupted.

"Well, you know that Cayce was a psychic. His Source was the prophetic speaker that shared knowledge with him—his Spirit Guide as he or she might be called today." I stopped momentarily to be sure Norm was listening.

"Continue," Norm said.

"Cayce was told by his Source that Jesus came through the line of the Essenes."

"I have read that. But how is that connected with the Dead Sea Scrolls?"

"Cayce knew this information ten years prior to the discovery of the Dead Sea Scrolls! The scrolls verify Cayce's information regarding Jesus' connection to the Essenes. And our dear Mary Ann aka George Eliot was researching the connection of Jesus with the Essenes shortly after becoming acquainted with the Brays when she was living in Coventry."

"That's interesting." Norm said without changing his inflection.

"I find it fascinating!"

"I don't know about fascinating, but it is certainly thought provoking." That was my husband. He never got rattled. He didn't believe in the overuse of exclamation marks. Neither did Lewes. George Eliot leaned on her soulmate for support in ways that he could manage. No other before him could do so. George Eliot was a strong woman in ways, but very weak in others. Eliot and I were happy to accept our men as the heads of household, but with certain understandings in place to allow for equality and individuality. Some modern women would shrink from the thought of allowing their husbands "head of household" status. Radical feminism had dented the armor of husbands, and this aspect of the movement's influence on culture would have been a sad fact of modern life for George Eliot.

"I will be home tomorrow. Is everything OK there? Are the dog and the cats being fed? Is the mail being brought to the house? Did you take the trash down to the road? Any calls for me?"

"Everything is just fine here, and no calls for you. I love you! See you tomorrow."

"I love you too!" The voice on the other end was gone. He knew very well that I was taking care of everything at home, but he needed to be reassured. What would I possibly do without Norm's micro-managing?

–18–

Eliot Conversations

I was *not* hearing voices, but Eliot's unspoken words were drilling me, inquiring as to when I would get off the merry-go-round of my life and push. It was *my* turn, after all! The playground of my life was threatening. I had to face Eliot head on, to learn what made her tick.

During Norm's absence, I decided to experiment with the "empty chair dialogue" method of Gestalt counseling, but without a counselor present. I had completed a study on this technique while I was earning my divinity degree with AIHT. I would "converse" with Eliot in the quiet of my own room. I would invite her into my world, and see what she had to say to me.

I placed one of my favorite chairs, the fan back Windsor, across from my desk chair. The writing arm on the Windsor seemed appropriate for Eliot. I draped a beautiful shawl over the back. I took these steps for me—to make the session feel more authentic. The more I personalized the setting, the easier it would be to imagine Eliot was really in the room. In the movie *Somewhere in Time*, the protagonist, Richard Collier, set the stage for his own travel back in time to find Elise McKenna at the Grand Hotel starring in a play in 1912. He bought a brown period suit and hat, and placed vintage coins in his pocket to spend once he arrived in 1912. He conducted this experiment in one of the guest rooms of the Grand Hotel, so the surroundings were very similar to those of McKenna's time. Brilliant movie! It was easy for me to stage my meeting with Eliot because the B & B side of our manor house was decorated in Victorian period style.

My first impression during the session was of George Eliot rearranging her dress, and then (in my head) she started the conversation saying, "Are we ready?" That was rather shocking for me because I thought I would be the one to open conversation since it was *my* session! But who was I kidding; this was George Eliot who would not fail to establish immediate communication? I leaned forward as though to take her hands and welcome her. And then I began to talk to her about my book and my intentions for having her participate in my "empty chair dialogue" session.

I'd written down questions in advance so that I would not forget why I went to this trouble to "summon" Eliot. I referred to my notes when asking the first question. "Why did you visit me in my library?" There were immediate impressions of what Eliot was feeling and thinking, though I did not hear audible words. She said that I needed her help, and that in her current state, she was able to bless others as she had been blessed with visitations when she was writing.

"You have lived a life similar to mine, though you were not challenged by the lack of fair physical attributes. You are kind, and sometimes you tend to be too kind and stretch yourself too much away from your own life plans. I am here to help direct you."

"You mean I'm to act as a channel for you?"

"Not channeling in your New Age sense of the word. I think there was a visitation of sorts from someone who wanted to help me in my previous life. Truthfully, I didn't believe in spirit visitation then. I do now. I owe Mrs. Harriet Stowe a letter of apology to say that I am converted." I sensed a chuckle from her. I'd have to do more research on that connection.

"Have I gone through this life reliving your karma because you didn't do something about it while you were living?"

Another chuckle. "You are invested in your own world, and you chose to do the things that brought you the unfortunate circumstances. The pattern was there for you to follow, but it was your decision all along. Say you purchased a carriage which was worse for wear, and decided rather than ride around London in a shabby rig, you would change the wheels and give the carriage a paint job, maybe add new brass lanterns and reupholster the seats in burgundy velvet. Is it the same carriage? Yes. It is the template re-covered. That is my life as a pattern for yours. Look what you've done with your opportunity in this life!"

"I see."

She sipped tea I hadn't served. I almost heard the spoon on the saucer! "You want to ask me how much I suffered in my life with George Lewes? I adored the man I called my husband. He was everything I had ever hoped for, and it was worth abandoning my family to set up housekeeping with him. You have had similar trials."

"Yes, indeed, I have! I am settled now, and I no longer listen to the gossip."

"Very good, my dear."

"I would like to heal myself of the wounds that are similar to yours."

"Your mother is happy for you, and says she might have been a distraction from your life goals had she lived. She would have stayed longer, but her spirit could not remain in such negative circumstances of the body. She is with you. At this very moment, you sense a pressure at the top of your head. Sometimes she touches your arm."

"So that's my Mom?"

"Yes, and others who are visiting."

"Why aren't others having visits from loved ones in spirit?"

"They are! They just don't know they are. They are afraid, and so they deny that spirits separate from their bodies at death. Therefore, they don't acknowledge the symptoms of visitations: touches, sounds in the room, feathers and coins, the scent of a loved one's perfume, butterflies sitting as though they are joining you for tea. Dreams are dismissed as well. They are as real as what you perceive reality to be."

"And what about my living relatives?"

"Your father is a simple man, just as mine was. He is very capable and proud, though he needs little in his surroundings to prove to others that he has worked hard all of his life. Be proud of him for who he is, and be there when he needs you. The relationship with your brother will not improve unless he admits his actions of ignoring you are wrong. In my former life, Isaac felt the same. He saw me as a fallen woman who had shamed the family. Yet, he attended my funeral, and grieved for me inwardly. Your oldest brother has already passed over. He was too sensitive for this world, and could no longer cope. You have sensed him. As for your younger brother, he is somewhat sensitive inwardly, but is full of bluster outwardly. One of you will pass first, and the other will grieve the loss as though there had been no separation."

"Will I pass first?"

"I cannot answer that. Just keep your heart open, dear."

"Will I be able to talk to you any time I want?"

"No. It is not up to me to come and go. There are restrictions on visitation."

She began to shift her weight in the Windsor chair. "Are they summoning you back?"

"I have work to do with others in need. I cannot stay. If you are receptive, I will come again. I am never far. You have sensed me many times through my writings, especially when you are comparing yourself and your life to mine. You are very much as I was during my youthful moments. Though your life choices have presented hard consequences at times, you have retained your inner youthfulness. Write from that center—write what that little girl has to say. Let the world hear you rejoice over the hurdles you've jumped, and let them mourn the early loss of your mother as you and I have done in the hidden chambers of our souls. All of it matters. All of it is important to soul evolution."

"Please do come again! There are so many questions I need answered."

"Time is a curious thing on this side of the veil. We don't sense it as passing the way you do. So when I sit down with you next, it may seem ten years to you, but an afternoon's walk along the Thames for me."

"That makes me sad."

"Yes, it is the wound of the motherless child. But know she is with you, and I will be close by."

The vision of her in my mind began to fade until I could no longer see the beautiful folds of her dress. *Was she the Divine Feminine?* I noticed no ugliness about her, and her skin was young and fresh! Perhaps this was her chosen appearance in the spirit. In my mind's eye, she was one of the Pre-Raphaelite subjects in a spectacular flowing dress.

"I love you!" I shouted as the session ended. I wondered if she heard me. My heart sank. It seemed I had a mother and a sister for a short time—someone who could share wisdom from deep within a metaphysical well. This grief I was now feeling was like deep loss: loss of Eliot, loss of my mother, loss of the sister I never had, or loss of self in relation to my family. Perhaps it was a multiple loss— loved ones from my soul group. It was shocking to "hear" Eliot speak of my older brother's passing. It was a deep hurt I rarely spoke about. But this session was meant to bring out the pain and help me work beyond it. It was less of an "empty chair" session and more like a visitation of spirit.

I turned away from the empty chair and went to my computer where I hurriedly typed all of the impressions I had about the session with Eliot. Until now, she had come to me in the pages of books, a being separate from me. But today I felt her in my heart and mind like a higher self, a spirit being somehow tethered to me.

-19-

The Open Door

If the energy doorway opened any farther, I'd fall into a past life! I couldn't imagine waking up to face George Lewes, or perchance see Eliot in the mirror. Nothing one could do would physically improve the appearances of the two Victorian lovers. Each discovery made me wonder if I might slip back in time and see myself struggling to look feminine, or stooping over the chamber pot in my new split seam pantaloons. Worse yet, how long could I cope with the antics of George Lewes? How long would he go on throwing up his arms, rolling his eyes, spewing Latin when perfectly good English would do, demanding every ounce of my devoted attention? Eliot loved it, but would I?

I have dreamed of parlor scenes where I sat on a couch and smiled as various characters walked by. The scene startled me awake shouting a rebuke only the Bible could offer up! Victorians had their potpourri, tussie mussies, and heavy perfumes to cover the unpleasant odors in the air. My modest white flowers fragrance wouldn't hold up for long in a house full of chamber pots and unwashed armpits. And to think I have owned a historical bed and breakfast for nearly two decades! I am grateful for modern conveniences in a quaint historical setting!

I know how make believe, dreams, and visions can set the tone for one's life. I was the one who was different from the rest of my family. My mind would go on wild flights of fancy. I play-acted these scenes in my imagination as though an actress on a stage. I wrote down what I imagined, and fortunately, I threw most of those writings away. Now that I am more mature, I realize, as Eliot said in *Daniel Deronda*, "Men can do nothing without the make-believe of a beginning."

George Eliot initiated "make believe" when she was young Mary Ann, creating scenes in her head and playing them out in the attic of the Griff House. In time, she proved herself in a world of educated men and judgmental women by holding firmly to what she believed. By acting on it, she changed the world—hers and ours.

The phone rang in the kitchen. I ran from the shower, dripping from head to toes. It was my friend, Jan. Before I could pick up the receiver, she had begun leaving a message. She said she wanted to pray for me, and then began a short but sweet prayer for my happiness and health. I didn't want to interrupt her in the middle of her prayer, so I allowed the machine to record her message. I would return her call later.

I had neglected my friends. I missed lunching regularly with one of my favorite cousins, but I had been too busy researching and writing to stay in touch. I had neglected my daughter too. Most of my friends lived at a distance, but sadly, I had not posted a single letter to any of them lately.

I needed to get away. I put on a simple black shift dress and pumps. I clipped a cameo into a scarf at the neckline before heading out to Easton Towne Center. On the way, I called my daughter to see if she could join me. To my delight, she was free and would love to meet. Brio was always amazing with its Tuscany décor and over-sized booths. Worn chairs of caramel colored leather punctuated the hall and foyer. I took it all in, savoring the feeling I hoped someday to have on a tour of Italy. Vicki was waiting in a corner booth. I leaned in to hug her. Was it the warm earth tones of gold and tan that made my daughter glow?

"You're wearing a dress!" Vicki said.

"I'm wearing a dress because Eliot loved dresses, and so do I." Norm seems to prefer dresses too. It is a touch of the feminine that some women have given up for the sake of comfort, rather than try to please their men. In Eliot's time, dresses were what women wore, but Eliot took special care with her wardrobe, and her dresses were made to order by a seamstress in her family." Why was I going on about Eliot? This was my time with my daughter. Eliot be gone!

"Did you tell me that Eliot was homely? So how could she get into trouble with men?" Vicki asked.

"Well, yes, she was homely, but she was daring. She took risks with her personal choices. She could do so with an intellect like hers. She was often among men—literary groups and philosophical think tanks sharing common insights. The average Victorian woman might be painting tea cups or tatting lace. I have learned, finally, from Eliot, that some things are far more important than others. In life, we must choose our risks wisely, or as you say, 'choose your battles!'"

"And what is important to you?" Vicki asked. She had a gift for conversation—for getting people to talk about themselves. I loved that! Most of the time people wanted to talk at me—tell me what they were thinking.

"Well, for one, my writing! I've been neglecting it for forty years, making due earning money by punching a time clock, being distracted by the opposite sex, and continually looking for my dream life, when it was right there in front of me all the time."

"Well, if you are going to pursue it, better do it now. You aren't getting any younger!" she laughed. "Speaking of not getting any younger, I have a gift for you." She dug into her purse, pulled out a coupon, and slid it across the table. "It's a coupon for a free consultation and x-rays for a new chiropractic center. You'll love the staff. They've done a lot to relieve my neck pain. If you are going to perch in front of your computer for long hours of writing, you'd better start your treatment soon. It's on me!"

"Thank you, Sweetie. I'll ring them up and get in right away. What a capital idea, and what a wonderful daughter you are!"

Vicki laughed out loud. "Mom, you're talking like a Brit!" I blushed a bit and adjusted my napkin on my lap. I guess reading all of those books, watching DVDs and making regular visits to Youtube to find videos on George Eliot had affected my speech.

The waiter came with our orders: Mezza Chicken Limone with mashed potatoes and roasted root vegetables. The natural lemon sauce on the breaded chicken breasts was a treat for the taste buds. For dessert, we enjoyed their vanilla bean creme brulee, a soft custard to die for. The chef had scraped fresh vanilla bean seeds into the bottom of the cup before he poured in the rich custard. I spooned around the ramekin several times like a small child getting the last drop.

"You are glowing, Vicki! And I see baby is coming along nicely! Do you need to go shopping for yourself or the baby? I would be glad to help." Already my mind was wandering back to Vicki's childhood. I'd saved some of the baby clothes from Vicki's early years just to remind myself of moments that passed too soon. I had some of her musical Fisher-Price toys to pass down to the grandkids as well.

"Thank you. But my friends have passed on all of their new and used baby clothing for little girls and big pregnant girls. No sense spending money on clothes right now. Babies grow out of them so quickly."

"Isn't that the truth? You are so blessed to have such thoughtful, generous friends."

"I try to be the same kind of friend to them."

"Of course, it *is* a mutual blessing. They are so fortunate to have you for a friend." I said that as though an inner counselor was pointing out the fact that Vicki and I had switched life roles. I used to be the soccer mom and the social butterfly. When Vicki was a teenager, I hauled soft drinks and pizzas to cheerleading practice and football games, and made friends all along the way. I was the mother who dashed off to school plays, concerts, and art displays at the mall. Vicki was my best friend, and her friends were my friends, perhaps because I'd spent many years as a single mom with her. We laughed and cried together, we went to the theater, out to dinner, redecorated rooms a dozen times. Most of our holidays were spent together at home because of family rifts.

When she left home after high school, I felt as though my life was over. She had always been there. Now others were making her happy—giving her what she needed for her life. That was a blessing for her and me, but there was a deep sense of loss when I knew she would not return to the nest. My life had been so full of fun experiences. Now? Now I was in my office almost every waking moment writing about some Victorian author and putting off my family and friends. Yes, Vicki's friends *were* blessed to have her.

"Mom?"

"Yes? Oh, I was just remembering all of the fun we used to have when you lived at home."

"Well, now you have me and C. J. and soon there will be another little grandchild to fill up your life!"

"That's right! Have you decided on the name yet?"

"I've always loved the name Gigi, so I think I will stick with that, and maybe the family can help us think of a middle name that complements it."

"How sweet! Can I get back to you on that?"

"Sure! We have a few months yet." Vicki's eyes twinkled, showing her excitement about having a little girl this time. "I will probably have to close up the sweet shop now."

"Yes, you probably will. I'm sorry. It has been a great outlet for you, and a gathering place for your close-knit community."

"Well, I'd better run so that I can get home to relieve Todd. He's watching C. J. for me today. Tell Norm I said hello!"

"Tell Todd hello for me, and thanks for giving you a break today so that we could have lunch and chat." She hugged me from the side, and turned to wave goodbye. Our meeting was over too quickly. It was all I could do not to weep.

On my drive home, I noted that the leaves were beginning to turn a soft red. Autumn was sneaking into the area gently—just the way I liked the seasons to change. Easy transitions. My favorite antique shop was on the route home. I stopped to look for an old book or two. Making my way beyond the cowbell on the door, and a hearty greeting of cheer from the register desk, I moved toward the back to find the vintage and rare books. Along the way, I noticed several daguerreotype photos of children with big eyes and sober Victorian expressions. There were stereo-optic viewers, and stacks of post cards and letters yellowed with time. I lifted one of the stacks of letters tied neatly with a pink satin ribbon. The handwriting looked as though it had been created with a fountain pen in a sweeping cursive style from the 1800s. There was a postmark, but it was smeared. The inside and return addresses were still very legible. The feel of the paper between my fingers was almost sensuous. The ribbon was softer yet, holding the letters like a lover's arms. *What dreams were inside these letters—what lives depended on the connection they provided?*

"Can I help you with anything?" asked the voice from behind the desk.

I set the letters back on the silver tray where I'd found them, and said, "No thank you. Just looking." I moved to the rear of the shop, and found a quiet corner. There were books on tables and crammed into shelves. My eyes followed a crack in the wall up to the ceiling's height, about twelve feet. By the looks of the crack, it appeared to be horsehair plaster covering the walls. I thumbed my way through the books on the bottom shelves finding *Oliver Cromwell: A Play*, a first edition dating back to 1921, and *Memoirs of Marie Antoinette*, published in 1890. But the prize was the last I put my hands on, *Lord Byron in His Letters,* dated 1927.

My paternal family lineage came through a sept of the Gordon clan. I had always been curious about George Gordon, Lord Byron. I saw a rather dark movie about the Romantic period poets once. Byron was a depressed, angry character in the film. He invited guests to his estate, drank heavily, and dumped his load of emotional pain on them. He was often in the depths of despair from which only his beloved dogs could shake him. I read somewhere that Byron had dozens of lovers. He had low self-esteem because of his physical disability, a club foot. Though his mind was brilliant, and that alone would have measured him as a leader among men, he was self-conscious about his physical defect. Perhaps that is why he had to prove himself with lovers.

I tucked the book under my arm and made my way to the register.

"Oh, you have selected a gem!" the cashier said. She gently removed the sale sticker and pointed out the frontispiece containing a portrait of Lord Byron protected by a vellum page. She gasped and touched the page edges as though mesmerized.

"Yes, I saw that. It makes the edition even more valuable," I said.

"Oh yes," she said, handing the package tied with rafia over the counter as though it were worth its weight in gold. "Enjoy!"

"I will certainly do that."

I smiled at her, and headed out of the door, stopping to take note of a triptych of the Virgin Mary and the Christ

Child. It was lovely, but I kept walking. I knew I would regret not making it my own.

The trip home offered nothing unusual, and my mind drifted off to the Romantic poets as my hands commanded the wheel—almost on automatic pilot.

Norm was home, and he was probably worried. I rarely went out without him.

"Hello dear, I've been worried."

"Yes, sorry. I drove to Easton and had lunch with Vicki. How silly of me not to leave a note for you!"

"How's she doing?"

"She's her usual spunky self."

"What do you have there?"

"*Lord Byron in His Letters!*"

"Uh oh."

"What?" I asked.

"Please tell me you won't start obsessing over Byron now."

"Oh, no. It's just that I've always been fascinated by his work."

"Yes, and you are fascinated with Eliot's work, and before her, Austen."

"Relax. I'm sold on Eliot, and committed to finishing my book. It is a book that is needed in our day and age. If the subject of reincarnation had been more acceptable in Eliot's time, she would have written this book instead of me." I held out the peace offering of Byron to Norm. It felt as though I were handing over a newborn baby.

"Look, it has Byron's portrait with a vellum overlay!" He sounded much like the cashier at the antique shop. "How much?" he asked.

"Twenty five dollars."

"Not too bad." Norm didn't mind spending money on books. I smiled to myself as he sat down in his tweed chair and began to browse between the covers. Just then he was the picture of the character, Casaubon, in *Middlemarch*! We teased each other on occasion about our mutual likenesses to Edward and Dorothea Casaubon. Of course Norm was Edward through and through with his collections of scholarly books and writings. I emulated Dorothea and was much like her as housewife, companion, and assistant editor of my husband's writings. And like Dorothea, I wanted to be of some good to the world—to reach out and improve the lives of others through my writing.

"Vicki gave me a coupon for a free consultation and x-rays at a local chiropractic center."

"Will you use it?"

"Most definitely! I'll call later. I'm off to make supper." There was no response. Norm was deep in concentration propping his feet on the Queen Anne style footstool. I had made his evening, and that wasn't hard to do with the right book.

Following supper, I left a message on the answering machine at the chiropractic center, hoping to get a quick appointment the following morning. Vicki was right; I had neck and shoulder pain, and I was taking too much over-the-counter pain medication daily. Otherwise, I was fairly healthy. I exercised, drank plenty of water, and ate fruits and vegetables daily. It made me feel good that people thought I was younger than my fifty something years. I wondered how Eliot looked with graying hair. She lived to the age of sixty one. In Victorian times, that would probably be considered elderly. Eliot was in poor health most of her adult life. She had kidney problems like her father. It must have been eerie for Mary Ann to watch her father die of kidney disease, fearing she might suffer the same fate.

Looking for my own gem to read that evening, I found another book on my shelf that was filled with wonderful stories about reincarnation: *One Soul, Many Lives* by Roy Stemman. I nestled down for the night, clipped a book light to the top of the lovely cover, and absorbed. According to Stemman, half of the world's population believed in reincarnation. Several of the stories were just downright fascinating. One of my favorites was about General Patton who said he had lived another life as one of Caesar's Legionaires. When a guide was driving him around Langres, France, (touring Roman ruins) preparing him for his first command, he told the guide he already knew the area, showed him the way, and pointed out the places he was already familiar with because he'd been there before. Patton had not visited the area in his current lifetime.

Stemman included stories about the composers, Mahler and Wagner, who both believed in reincarnation. There were stories of modern-day celebrities—some who just "knew," and others who had had readings to reveal they were reincarnated. Among them were: Sylvester Stallone, Englebert Humperdinck, Henry Mancini, and Loretta Swit. In addition, there was a chapter on past life regression and therapy. I'd already had my session with Dr. Cohen, so I decided to read that chapter later. It was going to be a good night sleuthing for clues among the stacks of books. My office was a mess, but Einstein's office had been messy too. Whose eyes would see it anyway? I had to have one comfortable room in which to wallow like a lazy cat in a darning basket. Norm padded up the stairs to his office. I walked across the hall to tell him goodnight.

"The book—the book. It is always the best company," he declared as he held up the volume of Byron's letters.

"Whatever you say, Norm. You may keep the book of Byron's letters on one condition."

"What's that?"

"You can't obsess over it." Without another word I walked out of his room, feeling his eyes riveting me from behind. I smiled to myself as Austen's Elizabeth (Lizzy) Bennett must have smiled when she pulled off a good one on Mr. Darcy. Eliot and Lewes must have had the same teasing habits to keep their relationship fun.

I tucked into bed and listened to my iPod play itself down. It was after 1:00 a.m., but I was restless and couldn't sleep. I counted backwards and drifted off in meditation. There was a door that seemed to be opening in my mind—offering a brighter light than what the night light in my room offered. I saw something, then fell fast asleep. The next morning, I lay in bed trying to remember what I'd dreamed. All I could remember was the doorway and the light. Perhaps I had been deliriously sleepy.

I'd seen doorways in dreams before—the one that was opened for me at the top of a castle staircase as Christ walked with me upward. Then there was the green door which opened and began to move back and forth as though the door was speaking. A strange language emitted from it, but I could not understand the language. The door suddenly slammed shut, and I begged for it to allow me another chance to understand. The door reopened, started moving again, and once more came the strange language. I remembered nothing more of the dream. Another doorway dream involved my Uncle Albert who had passed many years before. I knew him as a kind, gentle man. I dreamed someone was rearranging a toy train on its tracks in my room. The person stood and started walking out of the door. I thought it was my father, so I spoke to him. "Dad, where are you going?" The man turned, and at that moment, I saw that it was not my father, but my Uncle Albert. He did not speak to me, but turned and walked through the door, closing it behind him.

The doorway dreams began when I was around six years old. I awoke in the middle of the night screaming in terror after seeing a dark figure walking through the front door of our home. Not long afterward, my quilt went missing in the middle of the night. I blamed my prankster brothers, and went to their bedroom and demanded to know where they hid my quilt. They were fast asleep. When my father and stepmother heard the commotion, they came running. They searched for my quilt, but found nothing. I was given a blanket, and returned to bed. The last thing I remember was my father switching on the porch light to see if all was well outdoors. He seemed shocked about something, and turned to me to say, "Freda, were you outside?"

"No, Dad. I've been in bed." He looked down and tested the lock. He turned to me again and said, "Your quilt is on the pump house." I still get chills telling the story. Apparently, I had unlocked the door, walked outside carrying my quilt, and left it out on the pump house when I went back indoors. What I cannot figure out is how I unlocked the door and locked it again never consciously realizing what I was doing. My parents' bedroom was just two steps from that outside door, and neither of them heard me go in or out. Dad called it sleepwalking, but I've often wondered if it was someone else who carried my quilt outdoors.

The door and doorway are classic symbols in dream interpretation. They represent moving into higher consciousness, especially if there is light coming through the open doorway. I was beginning to see that all of the symbols, both conscious and subconscious were part of the story of my existence—a series of doorways through which I had passed to become who I am today. The final key was Eliot.

How could I overcome her karma and mine, and move on through that last door that the Christ had already shown me?

–20–

Healing

D id I sleep last night? Was that a zombie in my bed? I thought of the times as a child that I'd stayed up too late watching Chiller Theater. When I finally got to bed, Frankenstein, Werewolf, Mummy, Dracula, and Godzilla went with me! And when I awoke, I resembled them too! No amount of Cover Girl make up could hide the black circles under my eyes. I needed rest then—and now. I needed to free myself of emotional "monsters." As a youth, I would saddle up Buster, my chestnut barrel racer, and let my hair fly as I raced through the back fields. If only Buster were here now.

It was a new day, and it would end before I knew it. I was pressed to complete my book. I maneuvered my way up the narrow back stairs to my office and shut the door behind me, just as Eliot had done thousands of times. I knuckled down to writing about my favorite subject—the life of George Eliot. I was still confused, still asking myself why Eliot revealed herself to me. *What was the ultimate reason she risked showing herself in the library that evening?* I thumbed through some old correspondences from Dr. Heinemann to trigger my thoughts in the right direction. He was always good for a dose of wisdom:

> Never lose track of what is important here–and that is that many people learn, through your life's experiences, insights pertaining to their own lives. This will help them find their purpose, grow in consciousness...and this will be beneficial to all. That's the greater picture.

It was almost as if I had known him before—perhaps in another lifetime; perhaps in Eliot's lifetime. Suddenly my attention was drawn to my favorite biography keeping company with other books on my shelf. I pulled it down to have another look. The photographs mesmerized me. The book was concise with ample margins in which I could make reference notes. Why had Marghanita Laski chosen to write about Eliot? I looked her up on Wikipedia. The article indicated that she had been an avowed atheist. Eliot was a Christian in her early life, but later became a "free thinker" after the influence of Auguste Comte, the originator of sociology and positivism. Eliot was not following the church practices at the end of her life as she had while living with her father. However, Laski mentioned in her *George Eliot* biography that when Eliot passed away there was a copy of Thomas á Kempis' *De Imitatione Christi, The Imitation of Christ,* and her Bible at her bedside. That spoke volumes to me. She may not have believed the biblical miracles as a whole, but she did believe in the wisdom and healing that Jesus brought to mankind.

George Eliot was of like mind with some of the wisest people in recent centuries. Thomas Jefferson, the famous author of the Declaration of Independence, also wrote a "Bible"—*The Jefferson Bible*, which included accounts of the moral life of Jesus, but none of the miracles or the resurrection. Jefferson literally cut through a Holy Bible with a razor and glued the sections from the New Testament into a book format that left only the references that he preferred. I was shocked when I first encountered the narrow volume at a local college bookstore. This was not the sweet remembrance of Jefferson I read about in elementary school history books. DNA evidence also suggests that he fathered children with one of his slaves. He was accused during his lifetime, but never confessed. And yet, as our third president, he was and is one of the most revered men in U.S. history. Anyone who has stood inside the Jefferson Memorial in Washington, D.C. can identify with the feeling of being in awe—dwarfed by the mammoth statue of Thomas Jefferson.

Americans readily acknowledge the greatness of the man who introduced "We hold these truths to be self-evident that all men are created equal....," but they are slow to identify his human frailties that place him in the karmic soup with the rest of us. Yet, it is not his weakness that we fail to identify, but our own. We somehow forgive the moral shortcomings of those who have contributed significantly to our wellbeing, but we have less consideration for those who have not. I wondered how many of our nation's founders were moral in speech, and immoral in body and spirit. If these larger-than-life men succumbed to temptation, why did we raise such a high bar for the rest of us—for Eliot, for ourselves? Were we all hypocrites for not applying love and forgiveness to all as Jesus had done?

I think that Eliot tried to see the greater good in spite of others' shortcomings. She made her way through a difficult life—with her father, with her brother, with Spencer, with Chapman, with certain literary critics who read her books hungrily and then criticized her at the denouement. Eliot dared to do what they could not for lack of courage and unwillingness to face the consequences. They all wanted to be Eliot in deed, but lacked the fortitude. Most of her critics were male, so chauvinism could have been at the root of their diatribes against her. Most men of the nineteenth century wanted to keep women in their place. If George Eliot had not met the free-thinking Brays, and subsequently Spencer and Lewes, she might have played out her life's role like her character, Dorothea, in *Middlemarch*—stuck in a bad marriage where there was a dominant male who did not allow her independent thought.

Eliot had a lot of friends in spite of her social risk-taking. With her thirst for knowledge and truth, how could she resist the ones who dared challenge provincial order? The thought sent me leafing once again through Laski's book to find a picture of Charles Bray. There was a cameo of him. I was dumbfounded at what I saw. He looked much like Klaus! Or Klaus resembled him! *Why hadn't I noticed it before?*

Eliot was also an admirer of Heinrich Heine, author and poet, whose lyrics inspired several famous nineteenth century composers. The similarity in name and occupation seemed more than a mere coincidence. Heine spent most of his life abroad though he was born in Germany. The story elements seemed to be knitting themselves together into some fantastical plot! My friends, the Heinemanns, were born in Germany and moved to the United States to pursue careers. Perhaps the Heinemanns were in my "soul group." *Had we traveled together to be reborn in a circle of fellow souls, working out our karma together?* What a fascinating thought! But right now, I needed to get on with Eliot.

My job, according to Klaus, was to share my life experiences to help others learn through my insights to improve their own lives and grow in consciousness. I'd tell my story and what I've learned as a result of the Eliot introduction into my life. No fancy footwork needed, just tell our stories side by side in my book. *But wait—was I good enough, smart enough, deserving enough to put the story out there?* I wondered if I could withstand the public criticism that would come of comparing the brilliant nineteenth century British author and a simple farm girl like me from the States. I'd have to try. Eliot would have!

I looked down at my wrist watch. It was 1:30 p. m. Time to leave for my chiropractic appointment. I arrived fifteen minutes early. The receptionist told me I would need to fill out paperwork that required personal identification. "Half an hour tops," she said, smiling broadly. I headed for the waiting area and began to write in some of the most illegible handwriting I'd done in a while. There were several pages to the inquiry. I handed the completed survey back to the receptionist.

No sooner did I park my things on a bench space than a handsome doctor with white hair emerged from one of the doors in the adjacent rooms.

"Freda?"

I stood and walked over to him. He shook my hand, said his name, and headed into an adjoining room with a clipboard and pen. He was a man on a mission to learn how he could help me. His warmth and professional manner told me I could trust him with my health.

"Stand straight for me, Freda. Now turn your head as far left as you can. Now right. Now left again. Thank you." He looked down at my chart and shuffled through paperwork. "I see from your chart that you have been taking over-the-counter pain relievers, Freda. How much, and how often?"

"So long that I can't remember exactly. Perhaps twenty years or more. I take three doses a day sometimes. Two pills at a time—regular dosage for adults."

"We need to get you off of those pills, Freda."

"Why?"

"At the rate you are taking these, you could suffer from liver or kidney failure."

"What?" I was in shock. My mouth hung open and I heard nothing else the doctor said for the next few minutes. Kidney failure! *Eliot's kidney failure?*

"Freda?"

"Yes, yes, I'm sorry."

"We will take the x-rays now and send you back out to the front desk. We are going to work on your neck and shoulder problems so you can get off of those pills. We'll see you three days a week to start."

"Thank you, Doctor." I was in a mental daze. I walked down the hall to the front desk.

"How'd your session go?" the receptionist asked. My face must have given me away. She leveled her eyes with mine and waited for my response.

"The doctor told me I had to get off of the pain medicine, or I could experience liver or kidney failure!"

"Well, that's why we are going to help you with your realignment to help relieve the pain so you won't have to take those pills. See you in two days," she said, pushing an appointment card at me like she was dealing playing cards.

"Sure!" I walked out of the office feeling like I'd just been slapped in the face. Kidney failure! That was exactly what took the lives of George Eliot and her father. Karma be gone!

On the drive home, I wondered if there had been some grand design in the fact that Eliot's life had been revealed to me that winter evening in the library. Had that design become more intricate when I got restless and took some time to meet Vicki at Brio the previous day? Perhaps part of that plan had been in play long ago, and materialized when Vicki obtained the gift certificate for the chiropractor's appointment for me. *What if the grand design had not emerged—would I have died of kidney failure?* My head was hurting, but I feared taking pain medication.

"What's wrong?" Norm asked as I entered the door with my head down.

"Kidney failure!"

"Excuse me?"

"The doctor at the chiropractic office told me if I didn't get off of the pain medication that I could suffer liver or kidney failure!"

"And are you?"

"Am I what?"

"Going to get off of the pain medication?"

"I don't have a choice, do I? I won't risk kidney failure! I can't believe a common pain killer could do that to me!"

"Were you abusing it?"

"I didn't think I was, but according to the doctor, I have been overdosing."

"What will you do about it?"

"I am to take these to counteract inflammation." I shoved the bottle of herbal remedy in front of Norm's face. It has Turmeric in it. I've read about how effective it is in relieving inflammation." I was talking like an infomercial, filling space I didn't want to fill with obvious fears and concerns about dying. "I have to keep appointments for the next three months to have my spine adjusted to help relieve pain and reduce my need for pain killers."

"Sounds sensible to me." Norm said, giving me a quick hug and heading for his chair. I was left standing in the kitchen like a frightened child.

That night, I wrote to Klaus Heinemann and his wife, explaining my latest bizarre karmic connection with Eliot. I ended the email with "Karma be Gone!" The following morning, the Heinemanns responded to offer support. Klaus reminded me that it was my choice to relive or evolve beyond the karma of a previous life—Eliot's life. I was in command and had been given a divine gift in seeing Eliot's life in a nutshell, and now it was up to me to forge ahead and build on Eliot's strengths, or fall into a karmic groove and face the chance of returning in another lifetime to relearn valuable karmic lessons.

I was blessed to have Klaus and Gundi in my corner, helping me through each step. They were another piece of the puzzle—part of a grand design of my life that had been developed before I was born. I imagined the Heinemanns to be much like Norm and me: a couple so in tune that before one spoke, the other knew what their mate was going to say. Their purpose and mine worked out like the synchronizing of clocks. I gave them a story and pictures for their new book, and they supported me in the writing of my own. The Swiss psychologist, Carl Jung, had much to say about synchronicity in relation to our connections with others. A quote by Jung says, "The meeting of two personalities is like the contact of two chemical substances: if there is any reaction, both are transformed."

During my search for Eliot, I learned many karmic lessons. By learning who she was as a person, not just as a writer, I felt better equipped to brush off the negative energy. Her emotional pain had led to bodily illness. My emotional pain had led to bodily illness. Rather, our reactions to emotional pain brought on bodily illness. As a result of early loss, and a subsequent dysfunctional family life, I had lived much of my existence in relationship confusion. What saved me was my introversion—my need to be alone to create and recreate. Living among rabble-rousers was like dropping Alka Seltzer into a still glass of water—there was immediate, intense agitation—melodrama. But even confusion leads to growth by virtue of seeking a peaceful environment to counteract the madness. One learns ways of coping.

Much of Eliot's life was spent in emotional confusion. She was the sole caretaker of her ailing father from age seventeen through age twenty nine. Her first serious romance was with George Henry Lewes in 1853 when she was thirty three years old. Imagine that! No wonder she practically threw herself on Herbert Spencer the year before. There is no question why Spencer quickly introduced Mary Ann (then Marian) to his forlorn friend, George Lewes, whose wife had conceived children with his best friend, Thornton Hunt. The few whirlwind years between the death of her father and the first housekeeping years with Lewes were years of rampant self-discovery. She was judged severely at every turn.

When her father died, Mary Ann was already a spinster at twenty nine years old. If she were to fit in with provincial society in the Midlands, she needed to become a governess or marry. She did neither. She changed her name and hung out with the boys. She defied rules of convention. She'd been raised as a proper young lady, and the guilt must have been overwhelming for her when she finally turned her back on the lot of them, and moved in with her soulmate, Lewes. In essence, she said goodbye to them before they said goodbye to her. She made her choice to shut the doors on the world she had known for thirty four years, and open the doors to a new world where she could, at long last feel like an individual with private needs, private thoughts, and private ambitions. Her world took wings against all odds. Why? She was old, but she was bold!

I, like Eliot, preferred living a fairly private life. My writing required solitary time, my reading required a quiet nook with lots of books for company, and my positive relationship with Norm, like that of Eliot and Lewes, required much space for one-on-one loving support. Thankfully, Norm's life required the same.

Another writer-heroine of mine, Emily Dickinson, chose to live a secluded life. She loved weaving words, and in her lifetime she worked her alchemy on nearly 1800 poems. She could not have done it without her private time. She adored her garden and drew energy from it. Her solitary walks among prized flowers and herbs were transforming for her. It was a magic space that opened to her each time she drew near. She would not have known that that magic existed without her need for solitary space. Uncommon as it was, Emily was content to remain at home with her father and mother. She had many uncommon relationships within the privacy of written correspondence.

"Common" was something society could look at and say, "She's one of us." But the spark of genius that is "uncommon" is what causes the world to look askance—to judge—to reduce all creation to a narrow view through a telescope with a dirty lens. But when one takes up the magnifying glass with the polished view, they see that the "different" one is the one who stands out, and that simply makes one "different" not worse, not better. Dickinson was different, and thank God for that.

Eliot was different too. The "I" in each human being was struggling to become—to make a difference. We have a set number of years to do so in our current skin suits, then we must move on to another in our soul wardrobe. A particular life might feel less than ideal, but nonetheless, it was ours to fulfill the purpose of evolving our consciousness one life at a time.

George Eliot saw fame in her lifetime, helping her to overcome some of the branding by family, friends, and literary critics. Her novels became so popular around the globe that royals sought her out, Charles Dickens wrote a letter of admiration to her after reading her *Scenes of a Clerical Life*, Harriet Beecher Stowe was a regular correspondent, and Ralph Waldo Emerson knew her personally and read her books. Eliot and Lewes were seen together in public concerts and lectures more frequently by their admiring public once her popularity increased. The public loved her novels so they could overlook her sinful life. It would be much like fans worshiping Hollywood stars today. George Lewes was socially adept. He knew how to operate a room. He was an asset to Eliot as they ventured out to meet the adoring public. With the brilliant author, George Eliot, on his arm, his popularity increased. Perfect!

Emily Dickinson never overcame her need for total privacy. She became more reclusive with age. During her lifetime, a few of her poems were published in periodicals. Following her death, Emily's poems were published in book form. Hers was a unique style—a daring message to the world to hear the "I"—the individual, the creation that creates—the divinity of which the Transcendentalists spoke.

I believe this to be the same "myself" which Walt Whitman celebrated in his poem, "Song of Myself" in *Leaves of Grass*. We, the creative beings that bring to life something from nothing, have reason to celebrate! We know we have divinity within. When we acknowledge the divinity within, we cannot help but notice the divinity of others—then the "things" of the world become less important in the scheme of one's evolution of consciousness. The living beings with whom we share the planet become mirrors of ourselves. The reflection asks forgiveness for wrongdoing. We cannot deny our own reflection. The judgmental self begins to realize that it is not judging others but itself through energy connections with them. This realization—this openness of mind—allows the heart to open, giving negative karma the boot. What is left for empty space that longs to be filled with love? Love, and good karma, of course!

Where did that leave me? What had I learned, how had I improved, who had I forgiven—myself? What about the past lives mentioned by Dr. Cohen—did they matter anymore? Yes, they made me who I am: we are all connected in the grand scheme of things. I have forgiven and released the karma from my past. I have forgiven and released karma in my present, and I have forgiven and released karma in my future. I have held the children who were me in the past. I have loved them, reassured them, and released them. The healer is still active in me—sprung from the heart flames that could not be burned away by the embers at the stake. This life has served as a vehicle for compassion—to nurture those children in my past who were stripped of their God-given right to be nurtured. What lies ahead is not a repetition, but a clean slate dictated by my heart.

Would I, like Eliot, become a successful writer during my lifetime—continuing to stretch myself to the world around me—to heal myself and others? Or would I be like Emily Dickinson, writing for an audience that existed only in the distant future? I believe one of the reasons for Eliot's introduction to my current life was to encourage my writing—to tell about her, to tell about myself, to share with others that they can evolve beyond karmic issues, and move on to higher levels of consciousness. Eliot's health prevented her from visiting the homesteads of U.S. authors she admired, but I have been blessed to stand on the hallowed ground of those homesteads. I studied these icons of "free thinking" and compared and contrasted their ideas with Eliot's through the use of the Internet. My birth in this modern time and place, with all of the technical innovations available to me, has given me a huge advantage. The fact that I have written, formatted, designed, and published my own book is something that would have baffled George Eliot. She would have loved such control over her own work.

Still, I was being called to continue my walk, my struggle for good health and wellbeing. I had, for decades, been attempting to rid myself of pain by using over-the-counter pain relievers that only masked symptoms and put me at risk for worsening health. I learned new ways of releasing pain—physical and emotional—yes, they *are* connected!

The holistic methods that have helped transform my life include: daily meditation, energy work, prayer, proper nutrition, dream work, chiropractic adjustments, exercise, and proper rest. In addition, I have made adjustments to the way I handle interaction with others in my life. I have learned to accept personal responsibility for my actions, to express gratitude for all things that help me grow in consciousness, and to forgive (release) myself and others for wrongdoing. I have learned to love instead of judge. That's what Jesus did. That's what Buddha taught before Jesus, and what Krishna taught before Buddha. Whether we think these men were just historical figures, enlightened men, or saviors, we recognize that they contributed significantly to the human race. When we read the ancient texts, we learn to glean what is most important for our own lives. I think this was where George Eliot was in her life—having researched many spiritual texts, she found herself holding certain truths from which she never parted. The woman who was scorned for her lack of morals was a moral-minded person with a real sense of what it meant to be compassionate—to love and forgive.

Having learned from Eliot, I could not continue to nurse things that had hurt me forty or fifty years ago. Loving and forgiving others was my gift to them and to me. My soul was learning, expanding, and becoming more conscious of itself as a divine being. George Eliot was divine too, no matter what readers may think of her and her behavior in the nineteenth century, she was a human being born in God's image—one who suffered much and felt unloved. Such pain damages a person. I know.

At the end of my stepmother's life, she finally told me she loved me. My father began saying it too. It was healing for all concerned. I have two surviving brothers of four. The youngest one stays in touch. I know one day I will reunite with the other. My eldest brother came to me in spirit the night he died. He touched my arm and told me he was sorry, then he was gone again. We had spent years apart. I am grateful for what has been given. How could I hold grudges when hearts had been softened? Deferring to the wildly popular Disney *Frozen* song lyrics which give the ultimate expression of release, "Let it go!" (written by Robert and Kristin Lopez, and sung by Idina Menzel as Elsa the Snow Queen).

Because I chose to "let it go," I feel younger now, physically and mentally, than I did several years ago. For more information on how to transform your life, please see the website for *7 Days: Manifesting the Life You Want*. For specific work on karma, please visit my website for *Karma Road: Walking Through Time*. Both web links appear on the "Resources" page of this book. NOTE: please consult a physician before undertaking any program for physical or mental self-improvement.

I have a strong relationship with Norm. Eliot was blessed to have the same with Lewes, though they were never married. My marriage is secure—something I'd always dreamed of. When Eliot did marry in the last year of her life, it was to a man who was twenty years her junior. She was married, but it was not to her soulmate. I have successfully overcome that bit of Eliot karma because I *am* married to my soulmate who is split down the middle of Lewes and Casaubon. Norm recently requested a photograph of Casaubon for his birthday! I did not disappoint him. He received several poses of the British actor, Patrick Malahide, portraying the eccentric scholar in the BBC version of *Middlemarch*. I signed his birthday card, "Your loving Dorothea."

Emerson said, "If nature is visionary and the world a place of interconnected events, then man must make himself." He also wisely observed, "No sane man at last distrusts himself. His existence is the perfect answer to all sentimental cavils. If he is, he is wanted, and has the precise properties required. That we are here is proof we ought to be here."

If Eliot is connected to my existence, and it seems she is, her soul is longing for evolution, and it is now my turn to shine—to prove that her life was a step up the ladder. My life is yet another step. George Eliot found the voice she needed in her lifetime. Now it was time to find my own. Sue Monk Kidd, one of my favorite authors, said in her book, *Firstlight,* "All personal theology should begin with the words*: Let me tell you a story.*" I have told you mine. My name is Freda.

Afterword

During the writing of this book, I learned the true meaning of perseverance. From 2009 through the publication of *Karma Road*, I spent nearly six years: reading, researching, writing, proofreading, and editing. In addition, I corresponded with Eliot enthusiasts, philosophers, agents, and publishers. Somewhere along the road, I put my manuscript away. The trail I thought I'd sniffed out so well had led to a dead end. I was told that *Karma Road* fell into two genre categories, and publishers didn't like that problem. The secondary response was that the traditional publishing industry was challenged and watching resources. In other words, they were paying their big name authors to write the books they wanted out there, and not investing as much in "unknown" authors. That was safer for them.

Over time, my excitement to share my story dwindled. Then I took action on my life. I joined an organization of adrenaline adventurers, and in 2010 I attended a retreat in Bear Mountain, New York. To my surprise, I discovered I could walk on broken glass, bend spoons, and break boards with my feet. I learned that I had to break through the thought of failure concerning the publication of my book. I wrote on a board, "Make Millions Writing and Publishing." If you are going to dream, you might as well dream big! Then I crushed the board with my right foot. It gave me a sense of success I had not formerly had!

Many years ago when I worked in sales for Scholastic Books, I learned that when you make a sale, you get right back on the phone and make another while your confidence is high. That is what I did! I wrote a motivational book, *7 Days: Manifesting the Life You Want*. It was published in 2011. That was my first "sale." I used my own method of manifesting that I describe in the book to continue writing *Karma Road*. There's an old Jesuit saying, "God writes straight with crooked lines." My route was certainly circuitous: the thrill adventures catapulted me from a rural Midwest farming community to Los Angeles to participate in a red carpet event. But still remained the George Eliot saga—the book was yet to be published.

In 2013, I fulfilled another dream. I visited the Midlands of England with Norm. It was not a thorough immersion in Eliot, but more of a carriage ride with ghostly friends, Emerson, Eliot, and the Brays through Nuneaton and Coventry, south into Stratford. A ride through time that would leave me utterly changed, just as it had changed Mary Ann Evans when she and Emerson shared wisdom words at Rosehill and later that evening during a shared carriage ride to a Shakespeare play in Stratford. That meeting—and the magical Cinderella carriage ride that followed--proved providential for Mary Ann Evans. Just being in the English landscape of so many literary masters ignited my soul to higher thinking.

Norm and I spent three days as guests at the Griff House. It was a haven for us as we put down our carry-ons and dropped into bed. We had Room 44 upstairs at the Premier Inn. The hotel and Beefeater's Restaurant had been added-on to the Griff House. The original structure had been renovated and made accessible to tourists who made the pilgrimage each year to see where the famous nineteenth century author had lived out her childhood and young adult life.

The next morning my husband was so ill that I feared leaving him in the room to have breakfast downstairs. While I was not sure of the nature of his illness, I knew it was not to be ignored. I ran tea and breakfast back to the room for Norm, and got him dressed for our taxi ride to the George Eliot Hospital. That's right: George Eliot hospital was just a few miles from the hotel! They ran tests and prescribed antibiotics for Norm. It took three days for him to spring back to his usual self. In the meantime, we dined in the Beefeater's restaurant with John and Lynda Burton of the George Eliot Fellowship, and toured Nuneaton and Coventry graciously escorted by them. They were expert guides to whom we are forever grateful. The managing staff at the Premier Inn were very accommodating as well.

I awoke early each morning to photograph and take videos of the Griff House, the out buildings, and surrounding property. It felt like home. The sturdy red brick manor shone her face out toward the tree-lined drive. When our taxi first brought us from the bus station in Coventry, it was as if the ruddy-faced house had expected us to come. We were on a quest for Eliot that had taken us from a magical moment in our own library to this amazing historical home across the pond. Griff House had as much, if not more, of a historical commanding presence as our own red brick manor back in the States.

Looking back now at the first moments I stood on the grounds, I had been filled with nostalgia, almost as if I were returning instead of seeing it for the first time. I soon realized that I must have been feeling what George Eliot felt for over two decades after her brother, Isaac, exiled her from the family. Mary Ann Evans, George Eliot, would never return to Griff once those bonds were severed. Decades later, there was precious little time to send a letter to her brother following her marriage to John Walter Cross. Having received his sister's post, Isaac replied to her upon the occasion of her marriage, revealing his acceptance of the union.

Finally, at sixty years old, Eliot was legally married and had her family's approval! With that done, she and John Cross set off for Italy on their honeymoon. Eliot died later that year without ever having a face-to-face reunion with her brother. I believe these intense feelings of loss and longing were spiritually present as I walked the grounds. At times, I had to stop and regain my senses—remind myself that I was not young Mary Ann walking out of the back door into the barnyard, or the grieving George Eliot who had been barred from entering the happy winding drive of the Griff House for so many God-forsaken years.

The emotions were palpable in particular areas, and orbs appeared in the pictures I photographed—at the front door, entering the courtyard of the dovecote, viewing the out buildings where Mary Ann would have spent time gathering eggs, fetching the separated cream for butter, and other sundry chores that were part of the Griff farm life. I wondered if this longing was a familiar feeling of my own childhood paralleled with the strong evidence of Mary Ann's own lifestyle. It was all too familiar.

My search for parallels may never end. It started with a mysterious picture in the library on a winter's evening, took me through a plethora of literary, philosophical, spiritual, and physical doorways, and deposited me on the other side having stretched every thread of my being. This life is a journey to the self, and that self can extend through several lifetimes. Sometimes the paths cross and beg for attention or diversion. But Dr. Heinemann's wise words were a steady sign post on the road to finding myself: "A past life is just that, and you needn't relive it if you choose not to do so. Accept what helps you in this life, and discard the rest."

We bring authors to life when we examine their words for our own lives. On my way to finding Eliot, I reunited with Emerson and Thoreau, philosophers from her time. Dickinson and Wordsworth read poetry in either of my ears. I glided headlong into the Heinemanns, Gregg Braden, James Redfield, Dr. Doris Cohen, and a dozen more from my own modern world. The Bronte sisters popped in and out of my mind, and of course, Jane Austen. I have not stopped loving her. I adore her irony—her depiction of characters who live provincial lives, but are nonetheless tempted by money and progress. Jane Austen endures in quiet homes of women longing to be Elizabeth (Lizzy) Bennett. She endures in the classrooms around the world where teachers still cling to the excellence of English literature. She endures even though modern writers have turned her characters into vampires for their modern readers.

And George Eliot endures. She is more popular now than ever. Why? She was determined to live her life on her own terms. That is what the modern woman seeks for herself.

Eliot's thoughts have woven their way into our lives, bringing radiant hope to a world in which women have just begun to find their way as professionals in our modern society. We must always endeavor to do more, to be more, to stretch the very threads of our being on the loom of the world.

Books are alive with thought energy—living depositories of soul interaction. The word "coincidence" cannot define the unfolding events of my life as they relate to Eliot's books and characters. The more appropriate word is "synchronicity." George Eliot lives on through me—through all of us in the modern world. We are human with our faults and failures, but we are also divine with our capacity for love, forgiveness, and for "rebirth" in all of its various meanings. We must reach into the past and forgive ourselves and others, endeavor to live as divine individuals in this present life, and project blessings forward to the next. It makes no sense to "dust" only one book on the shelf. We are all of these books and more. Read on!

∞

Photos

Photo 1: Norm & Freda at a local mill pond similar to the one mentioned in *The Mill on the Floss*.

Photo 2: Dr. Klaus & Gundi Heinemann.

Photo 3: Orb on *The Mill on the Floss*, 2009.

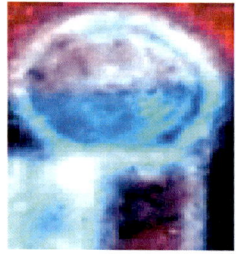

Photo 4: Close-up of orb on *The Mill on the Floss*.

Photo 5: The Griff House where George Eliot lived her childhood & young adult life as Mary Ann Evans.

Photo 6: The Chaney Manor, built in 1823. The porch and shutters were added in the recent past.

Photo 7: George Eliot statue in Nuneaton, with John Burton, Chair of the George Eliot Fellowship.

Photo 8: Nuneaton Library, George Eliot Collection.

Photo 9: Dovecote at the Griff House.

Photo 10: A bright orb with a defined interiority near the dovecote at the Griff House.

Freda M. Chaney

Photo 11: George Eliot painting by Granville White.

Photo 12: Holy Trinity, Evans' church in Coventry.

Photo 13: George Eliot's grand piano at the Herbert Art
Gallery & Museum, Coventry.

Photo 14: George Eliot's ghostly reflection in her vanity
mirror from a manikin facsimile in the drawing room.

Photo 15: Stonehenge on the Salisbury Plain. George Eliot adored the Wiltshire area and vacationed there while preparing to write her book, *Daniel Deronda*.

Photo 16: Stonehenge from our tour bus.

Appendix A

Quick Parallels List

1 The book cover of our Heritage Edition of *The Mill on the Floss* is similar to my *House Blessings* book cover, created in 1997. Both depict thatched cottages.

2 In the Heritage Edition of *The Mill on the Floss*, the picture of the Wray Manning painting of two females seated together near a window is very similar to the photo scene of the two females inside the glowing orb. The dark-haired lady on the right (in the book) is Maggie Tulliver, George Eliot's autobiographical heroine in *The Mill on the Floss*. There is also a dark-haired female on the right in the orb photo. As well, in both picture and orb photo, there appears a fair-haired lady who is older and taller seated to the left of the dark-haired one.

3 The character, Maggie *(MF=Mill on the Floss),* was a precocious child born into a family that did not support "high-thinking" in women, as was typical of the era. I was a precocious child, born into a family that did not appreciate "high thinking" at all.

4 Maggie *(MF)* enjoyed reading, writing, philosophy, religion, music, and art. In my youth, I played an instrument, and wrote poems and stories. I loved the philosophers, Thoreau and Emerson, read the Psalms regularly, and excelled in art. My family thought I was a nerd. Eliot fits the same pattern as Maggie, her autobiographical heroine. She excelled in reading, writing, foreign languages, and music. George Eliot met the philosopher, Ralph Waldo Emerson. He made a lifelong impression on her.

5 The character, Maggie, was so moved by music that she seemed to be having mystical experiences while listening. I am deeply moved by certain kinds of music in the same way.

6 George Eliot studied divinity, and translated religious texts. I studied divinity, and I have written for *Guideposts* publications.

7 Eliot and I have both had our challenges with finding the truth through strictly Christian means—being drawn also to mystical and philosophical aspects of divinity.

8 Maggie's brother *(MF)* received parental preference. My brothers were given preferential treatment by my father simply because they were males. It was the way of things.

9 Both Maggie *(MF)* and I are sympathetic to a fault. We put our hearts and lives on the line to help others.

10 Maggie possessed the heart of a child in relation to nature. The same applies to me. Maggie was fond of butterflies. I love butterflies, and have been blessed with mystical experiences involving them. In *The Mill on the Floss*, Maggie wore a butterfly pin instead of a fashionable brooch. I have a butterfly pin, ring, and costume I wear for parties and on Earth Day.

11 Maggie grew-up in the country and spent her days with her brother, Tom, who was three years older. Mary Ann grew-up in the country and spent her days with her brother Isaac, three years her elder. I grew up in the country and spent my days with my brother, who is two years older than I. Mary Ann, her character, Maggie, and I admired our brothers and enjoyed spending time with them.

12 The character, Maggie, *(MF)* was raised in the country on a modest income. She grew up in a thatched cottage at the mill. I was raised on a modest income. Our home was a Cape Cod farmhouse in the country. The author, George Eliot, lived in a farmhouse in the country during her childhood.

13 Maggie's father was a proud man and did the best he could. Others tended to take advantage of him. My father was proud and generous, often being taken advantage of by others. Both men worked hard, making their living off of the land. Maggie's father was a carpenter. My father owned his own sawmill and created skids for local companies. George

Eliot's father was an estate manager in charge of all practical aspects of land and building maintenance. He would have managed the stables as well. My father managed a Boy Scout camp for a brief time. He was also a tree-trimmer and logger, mined coal, and boarded race horses.

14 Maggie died in a boat rescuing her brother, Tom, who for years rejected her in his adult life. Like Maggie, I have felt the same rejection from my brothers. I was nearly killed in a boat when I was out rowing with friends. The story of that close call was published in *Angels on Earth* magazine and is mentioned in Chapter 10 of this book.

15 The character, Maggie *(MF),* and I both have dark skin, dark hair, and dark eyes. Our eyes seem to be our most striking feature. Maggie showed her emotions through her eyes, and many have said I do the same. George Eliot's gray eyes were her most striking feature.

16 George Eliot, and her character, Maggie, both lived in the 1800s when libraries and parlors were common rooms in larger homes. I live in a home, built in the 1800s, which has a library and music room. Some of the décor in our home resembles that of the Victorian period. As a matter of fact, even the floor covering in the Wray Manning painting of Maggie and her cousin, Lucy (in the Heritage Edition of *The Mill on the Floss*) is a similar color as the floor covering in

our music room. We also have lace curtains which are similar to the ones depicted in the Wray Manning painting.

17 I have made some unfortunate choices in the past, and have suffered greatly for them. George Eliot did the same. We have both had our dark nights of the soul. We grew from our experiences, and remained loyal to our sensitivities. The character, Maggie (MF), was sensitive—so much so that others couldn't understand her. As a child, I was sensitive, and had many challenges during my childhood and early adult life. My family gave up trying to understand me.

18 Maggie's (MF) father died when she was young. George Eliot's mother died when she was sixteen years old. My mother died when I was nine months old. Both Eliot and I suffered set-backs because of the early loss of our mothers.

19 George Eliot and I both used pen names. Eliot did so out of necessity. Typically, women weren't taken seriously in the literary circles of her time, especially in the novel writing genre. Both of our pen names tend to sound masculine. Hers: George Eliot. Mine: Noel Bleu. I had chosen Noël as in the Christmas song. Some mistook it for the masculine name, Noel. It is interesting to note that both Noel and George are used as modern names for boys or girls. I no longer use a pen name to represent my writing.

20 John Walter Cross was George Eliot's first lawful husband. My first husband's name was John Walter.

21 George Eliot's poem with the first line, "O MAY I Join the Choir Invisible," is very similar in theme to one I wrote by the title of "Harmony." Her poem shares a quote from Cicero to enhance the poem's meaning regarding the soul in the afterlife. My poem uses a quote from Don Costello to enhance the poem's meaning about soul. The first line of the Costello quote begins, "There is a choir loft in the soul...." See both poems in Appendix B.

22 Eliot wrote a novella titled *The Lifted Veil*, a book in which she shares supernatural experiences. Much of Eliot's work is moralistic, so it is interesting that she took a sharp turn to write a book about supernatural abilities. My friends, the Heinemanns, were featured in a film made for DVD with a very similar title: *Orbs: the Veil is Lifting*. This DVD led me to connect with the Heinemanns.

23 George Eliot admired a man who was a hunchback, Francois D'Albert Durade, the artist who painted a very becoming picture of her in a black velvet gown. Though it is hinted in various Eliot biographies that she may have had a crush on the artist, he was happily married, and there was no obvious romantic attraction between them. It is clear that Eliot had genuine admiration for Durade. In years past, I knew an admirable fellow who had a curvature of his spine.

24 Not only do I share some of Eliot's traits, but I have learned that my husband is very similar to her soulmate, George Lewes. Eliot and Lewes spent nearly twenty five years together and were extremely compatible. As of the publication of this book (2015), my husband and I have been friends for nearly thirty years, and married nineteen of them. We are soulmates and very compatible. George Eliot and George Lewes spent much of their time together writing, reading, and listening to music. Eliot and Lewes encouraged one another in their research and writing. My husband and I do the same.

25 In Charles Olcott's *George Eliot: Scenes and People in her Novels,* the author wrote that Eliot claimed her right hand was larger than her left from making cheese and butter at the Griff House dairy. I was in charge of churning butter with a hand churn when I was young. My right hand has knuckles that are visibly worn from doing various farm chores, not just butter-making. Mary Ann was the house manager at Griff after her sister, Chrissy, married. I suspect Eliot's right hand was larger from various farm chores and spending long hours creating hand-written manuscripts. I created several hand written manuscripts when I was young.

26 In the Laski biography, *George Eliot*, there is a notation about how Eliot held her hands "kangaroo fashion" in front of her. I hold my hands in front of me at my

waistline with my wrists folded downward (I have double-jointed wrists.) In primary school, my arms were long and gangly, and my friends used to mention how I held my hands at my waist.

27 George Eliot had a deep voice. It was one of the few things about her that others thought beautiful. I have a deep voice, and I have been told that I read and sing well.

28 George Eliot died at Cheyne Walk near the Thames River. Cheyne is pronounced "Chā nee" the same as my last name, Chaney. Cheyne, means: oak, oak grove, and oak-hearted. It derives from the French name Chesnai with several variant modern spellings including Chaney.

29 Eliot's death was caused by kidney failure. Her father died of kidney failure as well. I had kidney infections during my childhood. Recently, a doctor warned me that I must stop taking repeated doses of over-the-counter pain medication, or I might suffer liver or kidney failure. I have reduced my intake of pain medications by having regular chiropractic appointments, and by taking herbal supplements.

30 The Griff House in which Eliot lived during her childhood greatly resembles the house in which I now live. From the front, the Griff House looks like the front of our home. Both are two-story red brick with central entry. When our house was built in 1823, it had a simple front like the

Griff House. The columns and front porch were added much later.

31 George Eliot and I share a November birthday. We were both born under the sign of Scorpio.

32 Mary Ann Evans was Eliot's given name at birth. I began sorting through my genealogy records to see if perhaps there was a family connection. To my surprise, my maternal great grandfather was an Evans—Joseph Evans. Joseph was married to my great grandmother, Odecy, in the late 1800s. I am not aware of a direct link back to Eliot's family however. The synchronicity may only be in the name Evans.

33 George Eliot was considered homely. Her lack of beauty seemed to stem from her long crooked nose, long face, and large jaw line. When I was young, I was keenly aware that my face seemed too long with a prominent jaw line. My nose is crooked, and longer than I would like it to be.

34 Most of George Eliot's life, she preferred male company. She did not enjoy the frivolous conversations of most ladies. She could relate to men as though she were one of them. As she matured, she became an excellent conversationalist with male and female alike. As a youth, I was a tomboy, and spent much time in my brothers'

company, and in the company of their male friends. My best friend was a tomboy like me, and she enjoyed hanging around boys too. Naturally, I relate to men well, but as an adult, I enjoy the company of men and women.

35 Eliot began her professional career as a translator and editor. However, her first publication was a poem in a newspaper when she was twenty years of age. My first poems were published in a newspaper when I was twenty two. I began to establish a writing career by publishing articles in *Guideposts' Angels on Earth* and *Guideposts for Kids* magazines. In 2009, I began ghostwriting and editing others' books.

36 Mary Ann Evans was one of five siblings born into the Evans family. Robert Evans, Eliot's father, remarried when his first wife died. Mary Ann was the youngest child born to Robert's second wife. Altogether there were five children from two marriages. My father had three children with his first wife. He remarried after my mother died. His second wife already had a child of her own. My father and step mother had a child. Altogether in our family, there were five children from two marriages.

37 In the prelude of Eliot's *Middlemarch*, she extols the virtues of Saint Teresa of Avila. I also admire Saint Teresa, and wrote a paper on women mystics for my divinity degree (2008), putting Teresa near the top of my list. I once had a

mystical dream similar to Teresa's dream in *Interior Castle*. I was steadily ascending castle stairs to the top. I keep a statue of Saint Teresa at my bedside. She holds a quill pen and a scroll of paper in her hands.

38 In her early adult years, as recorded in the Laski biography, Eliot met Ralph Waldo Emerson at a gathering. She remarked that he was "...the first *man* I have ever seen." Eliot enjoyed philosophical and literary gatherings. I wrote a poem in the 1990s, "The Gathering at Emerson's," which won an award. The narrator in the poem is Emerson's house. A line in the poem described how the house watched those gathered, "I watched as boys came up to men, / and 'round about to boys again." I had admired Emerson since my introduction to him in senior class American Literature. I wrote a term paper on the Transcendentalists: Emerson and Thoreau. I have toured the Emerson house in Concord, Massachusetts many times, and I've stood in awe of Emerson's huge granite monument in Sleepy Hollow Cemetery.

39 George Eliot wore long dark dresses, most likely to fit in with men. She owned a black velvet gown she wore for a famous portrait by Francois D'Albert Durade. I enjoy wearing dresses. I own several black dresses and velvet gowns.

40 After George Eliot became famous, she and her soulmate, George Lewes, dined out in public together. They spent much of their day: reading, writing, and sharing ideas. They would work until the afternoon hours, and then step out for a meal. My husband and I follow similar schedules.

41 Eliot and Lewes were Goethe devotees. Lewes wrote a tome on the life of Goethe that is still selling today. My husband and I have long been Goethe fans, quoting him in essays and poetry. Recently, I found a hardbound copy of Lewes' *The Life of Goethe*. It keeps company with our collection of George Eliot books.

42 In addition to English, Eliot and Lewes both read and spoke German and French. In addition to English, my husband reads German and French. I have always been drawn to the French language, and I am learning it in increments in hopes of touring France. I used a French pen name for a time.

43 Two places that Eliot and Lewes lived together were Worthing and Richmond. Two places I have lived are Worthington, and on the outskirts of Richmond.

44 When George Eliot began her writing career, she edited for little or no money. She could not afford fine clothing, so her half-sister, Fanny, made her dresses. I have edited for little or no money, and quite often buy my clothing

at gently-used shops and vintage stores. Eliot was fond of the pilgrim collar. In fact the dress she is wearing as depicted on the statue in Nuneaton Square displays a pilgrim style collar sewn into the bodice. Though old-fashioned, the pilgrim style collar has shown up twice in my wardrobe in stunning, lace-trimmed pieces that I absolutely could not do without.

45 Eliot and Lewes consumed anything philosophical. It was Lewes who wrote *The Biographical History of Philosophy*. My husband published a comparative account of philosophers titled, *Six Images of Human Nature*.

46 George Eliot briefly studied experimental physics and used her knowledge to enhance her books. My mentor, Klaus Heinemann has a Ph.D. in experimental physics. I am fascinated by physics, but have never studied it academically.

47 Eliot loved the common, even in paintings. She was drawn to the Dutch painters for the depictions of common places and people. She was not in agreement with The Royal Academy of London who shunned the simplistic forms of the Pre-Raphaelite painters. I have always loved the simple country scenes, and especially the Dutch painters. My favorite Dutch painter is Johannes Vermeer.

48 Eliot was not in favor of the rapid industrialization of the English countryside. She included these strong feelings in her books, particularly *Middlemarch*. I have also fought

for preservation of small farms, rural countryside, and against industrial development, specifically in our area of the Midwest where farming is most important. I have written articles advocating for preservation. In my upcoming book, *How Divine*, I wrote in detail about my campaign to save pristine wetlands in our area from industrialization.

49 Charles Bray, a lifelong friend and mentor of Eliot's, bears a physical resemblance to Klaus Heinemann, my friend and mentor. Bray was a "free thinker" in religious matters, a political progressive, businessman, and philanthropist. He studied philosophy and published numerous books and papers about his findings. Dr. Heinemann has published over sixty peer-reviewed papers and many books. Bray had unconventional ideas about religion. The Heinemanns prefer a spiritual approach instead of a religious one.

50 According to an account I read in *Parallel Lives* by Phyllis Rose, Eliot's last drink was egg beaten into brandy (a curative used in Victorian times). She lapsed into a coma and died shortly thereafter. In her books, Eliot mentions the use of brandy for curing ills. For many years, I have made my own brandy from organic grapes. Although I am not a drinker, I do enjoy my brandy now and then. It *is* good for ailments.

51 George Eliot and George Henry Lewes owned a dog that looked remarkably similar to our Boxador (Boxer and

Labrador mix). They aren't the same breed, but still have remarkably similar markings.

52 When Mary Ann Evans was a young girl, she had "night terrors" frequently. As a child, I was also plagued with nightmares.

53 George Eliot visited Venice with her new husband, John Walter Cross. While there, Mrs. Cross made a special request of a painter. She wanted to see a particular triptych, "The Madonna of Mercy" by Bartolomeo Vivarini. The artist accompanied the couple to the Santa Maria Formosa Church. She was thrilled with the altar triptych, particularly with its pungent colors. I was mesmerized by a triptych of the Madonna, Christ child, and saints that I'd seen in an antique store in 2009. It was too expensive to purchase, but I've never forgotten it.

54 Young Mary Ann picked currants and made jelly with them. She also baked mince pies for her father during the holidays. I have always loved the tartness of currant jelly, and I make mince-filled cookies at Christmas.

55 In the museum at Nuneaton, there is a display of Eliot's personal articles, including a miniature perfume bottle. I saw no evidence of a large vanity style perfume atomizer. I have always preferred the small bottles of perfume, and in fact, I collect them!

56 While visiting the Griff house in Nuneaton, I walked to the old barnyard area. There was a dovecote that particularly caught my attention. I have always had a special heart for doves. I saved one with a broken wing by wintering it over in my basement. Come spring, I let it fly out of the basement window. I took pictures of the Griff dovecote, and in one photo appeared a brilliant orb with concentric circles (see photos of the Griff dovecote on page 245).

57 George Eliot was prone to chills, and was often seen nestling near the fireplace with her feet on the fender, or at her desk or window with her feet on a hot water bottle. When young Mary Ann was at boarding school, the one fireplace in the building had to be shared by many students. Mary Ann would huddle up, but could never manage to get warmed through. Eliot's final days were spent battling kidney failure. It was made worse with a throat infection (As a child, I had plenty of my own), producing chills that came on during a concert that she and her husband, John Cross, had attended. When I was a child, I suffered terribly from chills. Most of the winter I hovered over the kitchen register with a blanket wrapped around me to hold the heat to my body. I still get chills on occasion and use a hot water bottle to keep my feet warm.

58 I recently read in *George Eliot's English Travels* by Kathleen McCormack that George Eliot visited Stonehenge

and Avebury on the Salisbury Plains in Wiltshire. She loved the rolling countryside and wrote about it in *Daniel Deronda*. Before I became aware of her travels to Stonehenge and Avebury, my husband and I took a trip to England to visit Nuneaton, Coventry, and Swindon. Then we traveled south to Stratford, Bath, and the Salisbury Plains where we made our way to Stonehenge. I recall making our way through the Wiltshire countryside. I gasped as we began to catch a glimpse of Stonehenge from a distance. I jumped from the tour bus seat, and took a picture which I used to design one of the early working covers for *Karma Road*. I remember saying to my husband that I would love to live in that area. The towns were quaintly wrapped inside the curves of roads like children held in mothers' arms. I was in love, and it seems that George Eliot adored the area as well. She took residence there to write for a time, and inquired about purchasing land.

59 In *George Eliot's Life As Related in Her Letters and Journals* (edited by her husband John W. Cross), Mr. Cross shares that his wife told him there was a "not herself" which took over in her best writing. It was as though she were the instrument through which this "other" worked. She particularly mentioned the scene where Rosamond meets with Dorthea in *Middlemarch*. That entire scene was to have come to her at one sitting, and she wrote it down, never editing a word. I have had the same experiences where it

seems that words and passages are given to me. I have had entire poems in my head upon waking as though someone wrote it for me in a dream. In these instances, I remember getting the words on paper hurriedly so that I would not forget them.

60 George Eliot was very interested in astronomy. She loved the stars. She had planned a trip to the observatory just before her death. I, too, love the stars. When I was a child, I used to stand out under them for hours and marvel at their beauty. My husband is quick to point out the constellations. He built a rooftop on our pergola so that we could sit up there and view the stars.

61 Eliot loved long walks in natural settings, and felt her best while breathing fresh air and strolling through the wildflowers, naming them as she went. Like Eliot, I love the long country walks and wildflowers. I, too, have experienced healing in nature.

62 The Griff House, Eliot's home for over twenty years of her youth, had a long driveway with a circular turn-around area. In the center of the turn-around, there was (and still is) a yew tree. Our manor house has a long driveway with a circular turn-around area. There is a Yew tree at the turn-around.

63 My middle name is MAE, and <u>M</u>ary <u>A</u>nn <u>E</u>vans initials are M.A.E.

64 Using my elementary skills at Kabbalah Numerology, I found that my birth name has the same numerical value as that of George Eliot. Further my married name has the same numerical value as Eliot's name at birth.

65 There are approximately seventy three years between Eliot's death and my birth or three generations—exactly the number of generations between my great grandmother (who married Joseph Evans) and me. It is also interesting to note that Eliot began a serious relationship with George Lewes in October 1853. The year that I was born, 1953, counts one hundred years almost to the month of my birthdate. They referred to that fateful coming together as a "rebirth."

66 Mary Ann Evans was interested in Jesus and the history of Christianity. She studied to learn about the Jewish sect known as the Essenes. From her reading, she thought Jesus might have been influenced by the Essenes. I, too, have always been hungry for truth regarding Jesus' life. I have studied about the Essenes as well. It is plausible that this Jewish sect had a strong influence on Jesus' life. The Dead Sea Scrolls and Edgar Cayce readings about Jesus' life seem to point to that conclusion.

67 I am the namesake for my paternal aunt, Freda, who was stillborn on the same day (November 22) as Mary Ann Evans' birth.

68 There is an uncanny resemblance between Eliot's facial features and the facial features of my first boyfriend with whom I had a serious relationship. One of the gifts from this beau was a watch. After wearing it for years, the winding button had gone missing from the stem. I used tweezers to force-wind the stem for many years. Finally it quit working. One night I dreamed that he was stroking my hair. He said, "If I could only get through to you, I could help you." When I awoke, I remembered every detail of the dream. It touched me deeply because we were good friends when he passed away. Out of nostalgia, I walked to my jewelry case and found the old Caravelle watch he'd given me. I wound it with tweezers with no real hopes of it working. To my shock, it began to tick! In the following days, I realized that he had (or was it really George Eliot who looked like him) visited me and helped me cope in a difficult life situation.

69 There are 155 years between the time *The Mill on the Floss* (1860) was submitted for publication, and the final submission of *Karma Road* (2015). Eliot's book was sent to the publisher on March 21, 1860. My final edits were sent for publication at the end of March—almost to the day! If one were to take the number of years and convert them to single

digits, then add them together as numerologists do, it would look like this: 1+5+5=11. Eleven is a master number that cannot be reduced. There are only three true master numbers: 11, 22, and 33. In traditional numerology, the number 11 represents the pairing of heroic male power with the phenomenal intuition of the divine feminine—the mortal with the immortal—the physical with the spiritual. The master number 11 indicates that there will be a powerful breakthrough as a result of that completed cycle (155 years). It may be a personal breakthrough for me, and that would certainly be enough. However, the breakthrough could come to many as a result of reading, researching, and keeping an open mind. See *The Time Prompt Phenomenon* by Marie D. Jones ©2009 for more fascinating ways to look at number coincidences, particularly those coincidental numbers that keep magically appearing on clocks, digital radios, and more.

70 Since my childhood, I have used the slang term chintzy (see findwords.info/term/chintzy). It comes from nineteenth century England when the liberal use of chintz fabric was considered gaudy. The first recorded use of the word "chintzy" is in one of George Eliot's letters dated 18 September, 1851. She wrote, "The effect is chintzy and would be unbecoming."

Appendix B

"O May I Join the Choir Invisible."

∞

Longum illud tempus, quum non ero, magis me movet,
quam hoc exiguum.—Cicero, ad Att., xii. 18.

O MAY I join the choir invisible
Of those immortal dead who live again
In minds made better by their presence: live
In pulses stirred to generosity.
In deeds of daring rectitude, in scorn
For miserable aims that end in self,
In thoughts sublime that pierce the night like stars,
And with their mild persistence urge man's search
To vaster issues.

                    So to live in heaven:
To make undying music in the world,
Breathing as beauteous order that controls
With growing sway the growing life of man.
So we inherit that sweet purity
For which we have struggled, failed, and agonized
With widening retrospect that that bred despair.
Rebellious flesh that would not be subdued,
A vicious parent shaming still its child
Poor anxious penitence, is quick dissolved;
Its discords, quenched by meeting harmonies,
Die in the large and charitable air.
And all our rarer, better, truer self,
That sobbed religiously in yearning song,
That watched to ease the burden of the world,
Laboriously tracing what must be,
And what may yet be better—saw within
A worthier image for the sanctuary,
And shaped it forth before the multitude
Divinely human, raising worship so
To higher reverence more mixed with love—
That better self shall live till human Time

Shall fold its eyelids, and the human sky
Be gathered like a scroll within the tomb
Unread for ever.

This is life to come,
Which martyred men have made more glorious
For us who strive to follow.   May I reach
That purest heaven, be to other souls
The cup of strength in some great agony,
Enkindle generous ardor, feed pure love,
Beget the smiles that have no cruelty—
Be the sweet presence of a good diffused,
And in diffusion ever more intense.
So shall I join the choir invisible
Whose music is the gladness of the world.

George Eliot, 1867

Eliot, George. *George Eliot's Works: Poems,
Spanish Gypsy*. New York: A.L. Burt, 1910?

Note: For authenticity, the above poem was copied
Exactly as it was printed in *George Eliot's Works*.

Harmony

∞

The soul
The foot is wearing
Does not diminish
With the walk,
But springs on eager wings
To become
The hawk.

The soul selects a melody for two
Though heard by only one,
Bears the burden of truer sounds
Thrumming at the drum.
The natural ear
Cannot hear
A truth
As deep as this,
Betrays itself
With a single, silent
Hiss.

The soul
The hand is wearing
Feels the moment
To be thrust,
Yet lets it
Slip
With certainty
When it must.

House Blessings: A Book About Cottage Living

Photo Credits

Photo # 1: Norm and Freda Chaney taken by Vicki Lowery, US, 2005.

Photo #2: Dr. Klaus and Gundi Heinemann taken by Daniel Schmuki, Switzerland.

Photo #3: Library at The Chaney Manor with the original orb on *The Mill on the* Floss taken by Freda Chaney, US, 2009.

Photo #4: *The Mill on the Floss* orb with faces, cropped taken by Freda Chaney, US, 2009.

Photo #5: The Griff House taken by Freda Chaney, England, 2013.

Photo #6: The Chaney Manor taken by Freda Chaney, US.

Photo #7: George Eliot Statue with John Burton and Freda Chaney taken by Norm Chaney, England, 2013.

Photo #8: Freda Chaney in Nuneaton Library taken by Norm Chaney, England, 2013.

Photo #9: Dovecote at the Griff House taken by Freda Chaney, England, 2013.

Photo #10: Bright orb taken near Griff House dovecote taken by Freda Chaney, England, 2013.

Photo #11: George Eliot painting by Granville White, by permission of the George Eliot Fellowship, England, 2010.

Photo #12: Holy Trinity Church in Coventry taken by Freda Chaney, England, 2013.

Photo #13: George Eliot's Mahogany grand piano at the Herbert Art Gallery and Museum taken by Freda Chaney, England, 2013.

Photo #14: George Eliot's vanity mirror with black lace mantilla & reflection of George Eliot from drawing room taken by Freda Chaney, Nuneaton & Bedworth Museum and Art Gallery, England, 2013.

Photo#15: Stonehenge on the Wiltshire Plains taken by Freda Chaney, England, 2013.

Photo#16: View of Stonehenge from our tour bus taken by Freda Chaney, England, 2013.

Acknowledgements

Special thanks to my friends, Dr. Klaus and Gundi Heinemann, for their unfailing support throughout my journey of expanding consciousness.

Much appreciation to the George Eliot Fellowship for supplying photos from the Fellowship archives, and for the permission to use the painting of George Eliot by Granville White for my George Eliot slideshow on Youtube, for this book, and for the official *Karma Road* (formerly *George Eliot Lives*) book website.

I am indebted to Vivienne Wood who helped with specific edits for *Karma Road* in regards to George Eliot and her books. Her expertise enabled me to make appropriate changes for this Revised Edition paperback and Kindle versions of *Karma Road*.

I am grateful for my AIHT advisor, Annette Reynolds, who encouraged the writing and publication of *Karma Road*. She also arranged for and conducted a psychic study to assist me in the writing of Chapter 5.

Special appreciation to Dr. Doris Cohen, author of *Repetition: Past Lives, Life, and Rebirth* for her assistance in my past life reading session which led to the revelation that I *had* been a member of the Evans family in a past life.

I must thank Dr. Charles Ridley, author of *Stillness: Biodynamic Cranial Practice and the Evolution of Consciousness,* for his treatment and his comments for this book.

My gratitude to Brian Weiss, M.D. for his pioneering work in the area of past life regression. I am among millions who embrace his ideas about past life, and who appreciate his willingness to share his discoveries in numerous media formats.

Many thanks to my friend, Dr. Ken Atchity who was the first reader for my book in 2009. His professionalism, kindness, and patience has helped me to move *Karma Road* forward to publication.

My sincere appreciation goes to John Tintera of Duncan Baird/Watkins Publishers who believed in me and my book. His patient guidance made *Karma Road* more helpful to readers seeking to overcome their current and past life issues.

Special thanks to Alyce Chiles, Exec. V.P. of marketing at *Law of Attraction* magazine, who provided color "footprint" graphics for the interior design of this book.

Kudos to my good friend, Valorie Iglay, who assisted with the front cover photo sizing and with proofreading for the second edition and Kindle versions of *Karma Road*.

Much gratitude to Sunbury Chiropractic Center for their compassionate and professional manner during my ongoing treatments for health and wellbeing.

My love and appreciation go to my maternal cousins (and in memory of my deceased uncle) who provided genealogical and other historical information about the Evans lineage.

My humble gratitude goes out to *all* of the following authors and publishers below, and those listed in the Bibliography, whose publications have been of monumental help to me in researching George Eliot's life and writings, and metaphysical subjects—karma, reincarnation, past and parallel lives, consciousness, orbs—of interest to readers of my book:

Marghanita Laski's *George Eliot*, published by Thames and Hudson, was invaluable to my research. The Heritage Club Edition of *The Mill on the Floss,* published by the George Macy Company, was central to the story of *Karma Road. The Works of George Eliot: Life and Letters* (with John W. Cross) published by The University Society Publishers, and *George Eliot's Life as Related in Her Letters and Journals* (with John W. Cross) published by Houghton Mifflin were also extremely helpful. Jenny Uglow's *George Eliot* was beneficial, as well as Rosemary Ashton's *George Eliot: A Life*. I would be remiss not to mention G.S. Haight's *George Eliot: a Biography*, and his *George Eliot: Letters*. Haight's phenomenal contribution to the body of research on "anything Eliot" has paved the way for all of us who read, write about, and otherwise ponder the life of George Eliot. As for spiritual and New Age authors, both Roy Stemman's book, *One Soul, Many Lives*, and Joseph Head's and S.L Cranston's *Reincarnation: The Phoenix Fire Mystery* enlightened me on the subject of reincarnation. Sidney Kirkpatrick's *Edgar Cayce: An American Prophet* has long been a favorite of mine in the fields of healing and prophecy. There are many great books out there on the law of attraction: Rhonda Byrnes' *The Secret*, James Redfield's *Celestine Prophecy*, and *The Tenth Insight* open minds to the fact that thoughts are energy, and matter is energy moving at slower frequencies. Thoughts are things. We create our reality, our material world, with our thoughts.

I bow to all of the authors and researchers (above and below) who have gone before me in search of truth and understanding on these varied and fascinating topics. All references acknowledged here and in the Bibliography below apply throughout the book, including the "Quick Parallels List" in Appendix A.

Bibliography

Ashton, Rosemary, *George Eliot: A Life*. New York: Penguin
   Books, 1983.

Baker, William & Ross, John C. *George Eliot: A
   Bibliographical History:* Delaware, USA: Oak Knoll
   Press, 2002.

Blind, Mathilde, *George Eliot*. London: W.H. Allen and Co.,
   1883.

Bouyer, Louis. *Women Mystics.* San Francisco: Ignatius
   Press, 1993.

Braden, Gregg. *Fractal Time.* Carlsbad: Hay House,
   2009.

Buell, Lawrence, ed. *The American Transcendentalists:
   Essential Writings*. New York: Random House, 2006.

Bunney, Sarah. "Mr. and Mrs. Cross with the artist John
   Wharlton Bunney." *The George Eliot Review* 43.
   (2012): Print.

Cohen, Doris E. *Repetitions: Past Lives, Life, and
   Rebirth*. CA: Hay House, 2008.

Cross, John W. *George Eliot's Life as Related in Her Letters and Journals.* Boston/New York: Houghton Mifflin, 1909.

_____. *The Works of George Eliot: Life and Letters.* New York: The University Society Publishers, 1884?

Eliot, George. *George Eliot's Works: Theophrastus Such, Spanish Gypsy, and Poems.* New York: A.L. Burt, 1910?

_____. *The Lifted Veil.* Oxford: Oxford University Press, 1999.

_____. *Middlemarch.* New York: Barnes and Noble Books, 2003.

_____. *The Mill on the Floss.* New York: The George Macy Co., 1963.

_____. *Selected Critical Writings.* Oxford: Oxford University Press, 1991.

_____. *Silas Marner.* New York: Signet, 1999.

Emerson, Ralph Waldo. *The Sage from Concord.* Wheaton, Ill.: Theosophical Publishing House, 1987.

Haight, G.S. *George Eliot, A Biography.* Oxford and New York: Oxford University Press, 1968; Reprint:

Harmondsworth, Penguin Books, 1986.

Head, Joseph & Cranston, S.L. *Reincarnation: The Phoenix Fire Mystery*. New York: Julian Press, 1977.

Heinemann, Klaus. *Consciousness or Entropy*. CA: Eloret, 1991.

_____. *Expanding Perception*. Tarentum, PA: Word Association Publishers, 2004.

Heinemann, Klaus & Gundi. *Orbs: Their Mission and Messages of Hope*. California: Hay House, 2010.

Heinemann, Klaus & Ledwith, Miceal. *The Orb Project*. New York: Atria Books, 2007.

Hopcke, Robert H. *There Are No Accidents*. New York: Riverhead Books, 1997.

James, Henry. *The Creative Process*. New York: Thomas Yoseloff, 1958.

Kidd, Sue Monk. *Firstlight*. New York: Penguin Books, 2007.

Kirkpatrick, Sidney D. *Edgar Cayce: An American Prophet*. New York: Riverhead Books, 2000.

Laski, Marghanita. *George Eliot*. London: Thames & Hudson, 1978.

Lesser, Elizabeth. *The Seeker's Guide*. New York: Villard
Books, 1999.

Lewes, George Henry. *The Life of Goethe*. New York:
Fredrick Ungar, 1965.

McCormack, Kathleen. George *Eliot's English Travels*.
New York: Routledge/Taylor and Francis, 2005.

_____. *George Eliot in Society*. Columbus, Ohio: Ohio
State University Press, 2013.

Newton, Michael. *Life between Lives: Hypnotherapy
For Spiritual Regression:* Woodbury: Llewellyn
Publications, 2007.

Olcott, Charles S. *George Eliot: Scenes and People in Her
Novels*. Cambridge: The University Press, 1910.

Orbs: The Veil is Lifting DVD, Dir. Hope & Randy Mead,
Merkabah Productions, Beyond Words Dist. LLC., 2007.

Redfield, James. *The Celestine Prophecy*. New York:
Warner Books, 1997.

_____. *The Tenth Insight*. New York: Grand Central
Publishing, 1998.

Ridley, Charles. *Stillness: Biodynamic Cranial Practice*

& *the Evolution of Consciousness.* Berkeley: North
Atlantic Books, 2006.

Rose, Phyllis. *Parallel Lives.* New York: Vintage Books,
1983.

Saint Teresa of Avila. *The Interior Castle.* Trans. Mirabai
Starr. New York: Riverhead Books, 2003.

Stemman, Roy. *One Soul, Many Lives.* Berkeley: Ulysses
Press, 2005.

Uglow, Jenny. *George Eliot.* London: Virago Press, 1988.

∞

Glossary

Karma is the law of cause and effect. For every action, there is an equal and opposite reaction. I like what Elizabeth Lesser says about karma in her book, *The Seeker's Guide*, "Understanding karma motivates us to take responsibility for our actions. We begin to see that whatever happens in our life is the result of a chain of previous actions within the infinite web of all creation." She goes on to say, "It [karma] helps you to understand that everything that happens to you is part of an interwoven, ever-evolving, enormous and eternal tapestry."

Parallel Life (or lives) is an experience between two (or more) people who seem to be connected by soul aspects. They may live in different cities, countries, time periods, or dimensions, but they remain tethered energetically.

Past Life Regression is a specialized session in which a professionally trained counselor uses various methods, primarily hypnosis, to allow the subject to regress back to a previous life or lives in order to bring about healing in the current life.

Reincarnation is the recycling of the soul (following the death of the body) back into a new body to be reborn. There may be a time of healing and rest between reincarnations.

Synchronicity is the occurrence of two or more meaningful events that appear to be related. They are attention-grabbers, bidding you to follow.

Transcendentalism is a philosophy encompassing the core beliefs of the unity between God and humans, and God and nature. These core beliefs lead to a strong tendency toward individualism. For modern-day Transcendentalism go to: www.thetranscendentalmusicproject.blogspot.com. Also, see Philip Goldberg's *American Veda: From Emerson and the Beatles to Yoga and Meditation—How Indian Spirituality Changed the West:* www.americanveda.com.

∞

Resources

Website & Blog

Official website for *Karma Road*: *Walking through Time*
www.karmaroadwalkingthroughtime.com

∞

Video Tour

George Eliot video tour
http://youtu.be/2s8rZ6SdI8k

∞

Also by Freda Chaney

7 Days: Manifesting the Life You Want

Official book website
http://www.7daysmanifestingthelifeyouwant.com

About the Author

Freda studied liberal arts at Otterbein College and earned her doctorate degree in divinity from the American Institute of Holistic Theology. She wears many hats as an author, motivational mentor, and entrepreneur. Freda's writing career spans forty years. Her publications include: books, magazines, articles, blogs, and award-winning poetry. She is the wife of Dr. Norman Chaney, mother of artist Vicki Lowery, and proud grandmother of Carter and Genevieve. Freda and her husband share their historical home with their spunky fur friend, Rocky, who looks remarkably similar to George Eliot's dog, Ben!

Made in the USA
Middletown, DE
09 May 2015